Advance Praise for
The Two Hands of Yes and No

"My grandfather would be happy and proud of how the Linns have honored his legacy and carried on his work. This an important book for all peacemakers. It has a wealth of information, well researched and written, on how nonviolence has succeeded in resolving so many conflicts around the world. This book is a must read for anyone who has any doubts about the efficacy of nonviolence." —**Arun Gandhi, founder/president, Gandhi Worldwide Education Institute**

"All of us need to be grateful for the clarity of this exceptional book. The Linns have presented a hugely accessible exploration of active nonviolence that will be the 'go-to' book for generations to come. Weaving historical, biblical, and personal threads that not only inform but lead the reader to recognize 'love in action' as the fundamental architecture of our hearts, there is in this book and in the lives of the authors a 'boundlessness . . . that will make all boundaries tremble.' The holiness of our current resistance needs this book." —**Gregory J. Boyle, S.J., founder, Homeboy Industries, author, *Tattoos on the Heart***

"As practical and experienced peacemakers, the Linn family is unmatched in their commitment to nonviolent solutions to conflicts, whether large or small. Equally unmatched is the singular and persuasive power of the story they tell in *The Two Hands of Yes and No*. It deserves a wide audience." —**Colman McCarthy, director, Center for Teaching Peace, author, *I'd Rather Teach Peace***

"Unique among the Linns' many books, this one was written by two generations: Sheila and Denny, and their young son John. Unique among books on active nonviolence, it includes the psychological foundation that helps humans realize their innate capacity for goodness. Fascinating stories and surprising information offer hope to all, including John's generation represented by the Parkland students who are leading the way for a country in despera and determination. May this book be require school and college, and for everyone desiring next generation." —**Richard Rohr, O.F.M., C templation**

"*The Two Hands of Yes and No* brings active nonviolence into clear focus as a powerful and effective approach to transforming violence and conflict, even in extremely difficult circumstances. Woven into the many great examples of contemporary nonviolent action are deeper, crucial questions about what motivates human beings to embrace non-violence and how the human community might better prepare to move toward a nonviolent future. Thank you to the Linns for an important and inspiring book." — **Marie Dennis, co-president, Pax Christi International**

"This is the only book I know of on active nonviolence written by a family and the only one that includes the psychological foundation for nonviolence. The Linns voice the hope of parents and children everywhere — that we have the power to end violence, injustice, and war, and one day live in peace. They include the perspective of young John, who has participated in nonviolent action since early childhood and who represents a generation that has been mobilized by the Parkland students. And they include the perspective of Denny and Sheila, John's parents, who have worked for peace and justice all their lives. Along the way, the Linns give us all new hope." — **Rev. John Dear, author,** *The Nonviolent Life* **and** *Living Peace*

"This book is a life saver! The Linns show us how nonviolence works and why it is the path to our healing and survival. May *The Two Hands of Yes and No* reach new generations of peacemakers and remind us all of what is possible and how we can get there — together!" — **G. Scott Brown, author,** *Active Peace: A Mindful Path to a Nonviolent World*

"Gandhi said, 'If we want peace we will have to begin with the children.' The mainstream culture we feed our children today is precisely the opposite. Here, the Linns give us something healthier to grow on. This book has an extra note of authenticity, as it is told from the perspective of a family, including a young adult student. Packed with information about active nonviolence (a rapidly developing but still little known science) and compelling stories, reading it is an uplifting and learning experience, with exercises and reflections at the end of every (relatively short) chapter. I highly recommend this book for young adult readers and their parents." — **Michael Nagler, president, Metta Center for Nonviolence**

The Two Hands
of Yes and No

One Family's Encounter
with the Surprising Power
of Active Nonviolence

John Linn
Sheila Fabricant Linn
Dennis Linn

ORBIS BOOKS
Maryknoll, New York 10545

ORBIS BOOKS
Maryknoll, New York 10545

Fathers and Brothers
MARYKNOLL™

Founded in 1970, Orbis Books endeavors to publish works that enlighten the mind, nourish the spirit, and challenge the conscience. The publishing arm of the Maryknoll Fathers and Brothers, Orbis seeks to explore the global dimensions of the Christian faith and mission, to invite dialogue with diverse cultures and religious traditions, and to serve the cause of reconciliation and peace. The books published reflect the views of their authors and do not represent the official position of the Maryknoll Society. To learn more about Maryknoll and Orbis Books, please visit our website at www.maryknollsociety.org.

Library of Congress Cataloging-in-Publication Data

Names: Linn, John, 1997- author. | Linn, Sheila Fabricant, author. | Linn, Dennis, author.
Title: The two hands of yes and no : one family's encounter with the surprising power of active nonviolence / John Linn, Sheila Fabricant Linn, Dennis Linn.
Other titles: One family's encounter with the surprising power of active nonviolence
Description: Maryknoll, NY : Orbis Books, [2019] | Includes bibliographical references and index.
Identifiers: LCCN 2019008932 (print) | LCCN 2019012088 (ebook) | ISBN 9781608337972 (e-book) | ISBN 9781626983335 (pbk.)
Subjects: LCSH: Nonviolence. | Direct action. | Anti-Nazi movement.
Classification: LCC HM1281 (ebook) | LCC HM1281 .L56 2019 (print) | DDC 303.6/1--dc23
LC record available at https://lccn.loc.gov/2019008932

Dedicated to
the faculty and staff of
Vail Mountain School
and
Students Shoulder-to-Shoulder

in gratitude for holding our family in love and goodness.

When the opportunity presents itself for you to defeat your enemy, that is the time when you must not do it . . . when you rise to the level of love, of its great beauty and power, you seek only to defeat evil systems. Individuals who happen to be caught up in that system, you love, but you seek to defeat the system . . . hate for hate only intensifies the existence of hate and evil in the universe. If I hit you and you hit me and I hit you back and you hit me back and so on, you see, that goes on ad infinitum. It just never ends. Somewhere somebody must have a little sense, and that's the strong person. The strong person is the person who can cut off the chain of hate, the chain of evil . . . somebody must have . . . morality enough to cut it off and inject within the very structure of the universe, that strong and powerful element of love.

Martin Luther King, Jr.
Sermon delivered at Dexter Avenue Baptist Church,
Montgomery, Alabama,
November 17, 1957

My grandfather had a dream that his four little children will not be judged by the color of their skin, but the content of their character. I have a dream that enough is enough. And that this should be a gun-free world, period.

Yolanda Renee King
Granddaughter of Martin Luther King Jr., age nine
Speech delivered at March for Our Lives
March 24, 2018

Contents

Acknowledgments

The three of us want to thank the following friends and colleagues for their willingness and care in reading the manuscript for this book: Malia Barca, Mike Beerntsen, Kate Blakslee, Roy Bourgeois, Dylan Cunningham, John Dear, Kate Drescher, Marisa Ferrara, Julie Keith, Karambu Ringera, Sherri Steeves, and Fran Shure.

I (John) want to thank all those who supported me in my Vail Mountain School high school senior project, which inspired my parents and me to write this book. Kate Blakslee, Kate Drescher, and Maggie Pavlik are the faculty members who worked especially closely with me, and I will remember them forever as examples of education for kindness, goodness, and empathy. I also want to thank my history teacher, Doug Litowitz, and my good friend Hunter Meier for their help. Thanks to my mom, Sheila, for spending many hours helping me with this project. Thank you to my outside adviser, John Dear, for taking time out of his busy schedule to meet with me and my parents in Santa Fe, and to Roy Bourgeois and Hendrik Voss for allowing us to interview them.

Thanks to Sandy Vaillancourt for her generosity in donating her original cover art and to Michael Calvente for the cover design. Finally, we are most grateful to Robert Ellsberg for welcoming us to Orbis Books and to staff members Maria Angelini, Doris Goodnough, Nancy Keels, Michael Lawrence, Diana McDermott, Bill Medeot, Linda Mulvaney, and Bernadette Price. You live what you publish by exemplifying the kindness, patience, and spirit of mutuality that make active nonviolence possible. We feel very happy to be among your authors.

Why Did We Write This, and Why Now?

The three of us taught an elective class to high school students on active nonviolence at the school from which I (John) had just graduated. After a few sessions, one of our students, Spencer, wrote to us about the "magic of nonviolence." He sent us a video in which a man is leaving a pizza parlor with the pizza he just bought. He sees two men fighting on the sidewalk outside, beating each other with their fists. He offers his pizza to the two men, putting his arm around the shoulders of one man and then the other. The two men stop fighting, accept the pizza, and walk off in opposite directions eating it.[1]

That video and Spencer's words capture our reason for writing this book. From stopping a fight with pizza, to disarming a robber by offering him a glass of wine, to bringing down a dictator in Lithuania by forming a human chain across the entire country, to using flowers and food to stop the collision of two armies in the Philippines, to preventing the extermination of Jews in many parts of Europe, the study and practice of active nonviolence has given our family a doorway into the magical, ultimately loving nature of reality and an opportunity to share that with others.

John's Story

My parents, Denny and Sheila, first introduced me to this magical world when I was six months old. They brought me to

EDSA Boulevard in Manila, site of the 1986 Philippine People Power Revolution. President Marcos had stolen an election, and reform-minded military officers rebelled against him. The army of the dictatorial Marcos government and the opposition soldiers were about to violently confront each other. Millions of people swarmed the streets and stopped the soldiers in their tanks on EDSA Boulevard and gave them flowers, sandwiches, and fruits. Instead of a violent confrontation, the Marcos government was overthrown peacefully, and democratically elected Cory Aquino was installed as president. I was too young to remember that trip, but my parents told me the story many times.

When I was four years old, my parents took me to the U.S. Air Force base at Spangdahlem, Germany, where they were invited to give a retreat on nonviolence to soldiers. The chaplain who invited them said, "Soldiers know better than anyone the cost of war, and they want another way."

When I was five, we visited Le Chambon, France, the site of one of the largest campaigns of successful nonviolent resistance to the Nazis. The five thousand villagers of Le Chambon saved five thousand Jews (see chapter 9). I have a photo of myself standing in the pulpit of Rev. André Trocmé, the town's pastor, who was the foremost leader of nonviolent resistance in Europe during World War II.

When I was seven, I participated in a demonstration in Denver, Colorado, against the Iraq War, and my picture even made the *Denver Post*. When I was eight, my family and I joined anti-Iraq War activist Cindy Sheehan for a demonstration in front of the White House. This time I made the *Washington Times*.

When I was eleven, my family and I joined twenty thousand other people for the annual demonstration to close the School of the Americas (now WHINSEC) at Fort Benning, Georgia, where Latin American soldiers were trained in methods of torture. When I was fourteen, we spent three days in a tiny village in Guatemala with our friend Andrea, a missionary who saved indigenous leaders from being killed by the military (some of whom were trained at the School of the Americas). She ran a kind of "underground railway," using a jeep that my parents asked my grandfather to donate. Andrea took leaders from one safe house to another, sometimes on stretchers to pretend they were sick, so the army would be less likely to arrest them. When I heard the story, I realized that Andrea could have been killed at any moment, and I felt really stunned by her courage.

These experiences were possible because I was home schooled until ninth grade and free to travel with my parents, who gave conferences all over the world and wanted to expose me to a wide variety of people and cultures. Then I began formal schooling at Vail Mountain School (VMS), where the psychological qualities that underlie the capacity for nonviolence are emphasized. As a student there, I participated in service trips to a Nicaraguan refugee camp, the Pine Ridge Sioux Reservation, Cambodia, and Kenya. In all these places, I saw the effects of war and poverty on native people.

When I was eighteen, I did my high school senior project on active nonviolence. I called it "Satyagraha = Love in Action: The Power of Nonviolence and Its Psychological Foundation." My outside advisor was John Dear, a family friend, who has been nominated twice for the Nobel Peace Prize (first by Desmond Tutu). With the support of my advisers and my mother's help, I wrote a very long paper, I conducted an oral defense of my paper, and then I presented my project to the Vail Mountain School community. My project was then the basis for the class my parents and I taught at my school during my gap year, and both the project and the class are the basis for this book. As we were writing this, my parents and I visited some of the places described here, including Gandhi's ashram in India, the site of the rescue of the Jews in Denmark during World War II, and the region of Belgium where the Christmas Truce of 1914 took place.

These experiences have influenced me profoundly, as have

the people I have met or grown up with who have modeled nonviolence for me. My parents put me in a field of greatness by exposing me to courageous, caring people who had caught the magical spirit of active nonviolence. For instance, they took me to meet the historian Howard Zinn, who was a soldier in World War II and became a pacifist. He was an outspoken advocate for peace and justice throughout his life, from the civil rights movement to the Iraq War. We did not know him, but my parents believed that just by being in his presence we would catch something of his spirit.

The courageous, caring people I have been fortunate to know include my godfather, Paul Johnston, the former mayor of our town, who was renowned for his quiet good deeds. Paul owned a hotel—a rather expensive and elegant one—where he kept a room reserved for any homeless person who was found wandering around town with nowhere to go for the night. Paul was a soldier from 1955 to 1957. He became a committed pacifist after he was discharged, and he went to peace demonstrations with us.

Another caring person in my life is Walter Wink, one of the foremost contemporary biblical theologians and teachers of nonviolence. He was like a godfather to me until his death and, I believe, still watches over me. Walter's work on "Jesus' third way" contributed significantly to the relatively nonviolent end of apartheid in South Africa (see Introduction). I grew up with Walter and his wife, June, often staying in their home and welcoming them to stay in ours.

After home schooling, my parents sent me to VMS, because the school's priority is to support students in becoming kind, caring, conscious global citizens. Although my family is not wealthy, we live in a very wealthy community, and VMS has access to the best educational resources. I had excellent teachers there. Yet, I was taught almost nothing in high school about active nonviolence. I took world history and Advanced Placement U.S. History, and, apart from a chapter on the American civil rights movement, the emphasis was on who won wars and who lost them. I imagine most readers my age have experienced something similar.

My parents and I are grateful that VMS trusted us to teach a class on nonviolence based upon my senior project. But I want not only students at my school, but students everywhere, to learn that war is not the only answer and that it is not even an effective answer in the long run. The people I have mentioned above and my own experiences of active nonviolence have given me hope for my life and the lives of my children-to-come that we can find a better way. I want to pass on that hope to you.

Denny and Sheila's Story

As John said, we (Denny and Sheila) took him to EDSA Boulevard in the Philippines when he was six months old. Of course, we knew that he was too small to consciously understand why we were there, but we wanted him to be in the energetic field of the People Power Revolution. We hoped he would grow up to appreciate active nonviolence and share our commitment to it.

Beginning in college and for much of our adult lives, we have participated in nonviolent actions such as peace demonstrations. However, it was an experience in Guatemala, where we were invited to give a conference, that taught us the power of nonviolence. Guatemala went through a period of genocidal violence toward its indigenous people so brutal that hundreds of thousands were massacred, including entire villages. Leaders of the native Mayans were especially targeted, as well as anyone who tried to educate or organize them. During this time, our friend, Andrea (whom John spoke of above), worked in a small mountain village, teaching the people and helping them develop leadership skills. Andrea and her people knew they were risking their lives.

The people saw that the military used a strategy that is typical of oppressive regimes. Government soldiers would come into the village and use spies to find out who was angry at whom—in other words, where the feuds were—especially among families that included people with leadership ability, since the government wanted to eliminate these people.

Thus, for example, government spies might learn that the Garcia family was angry at the Reyes family because the Garcias believed the Reyeses took their land two hundred years before. The soldiers would then kidnap members of the Garcia family and force them to give false information about the Reyeses, such as that they were communists or guerillas. Then the soldiers would kidnap members of the Reyes family and force them to give false information about the Garcias. Finally, they would use this information as an excuse to take the leaders from both families away and kill them.

The people realized that it was the divisions between them, caused by unhealed hurts, that made them vulnerable to this kind of violence. Andrea asked us and Denny's brother Matt to come and teach the people processes for forgiveness, which we did. The people spent the next year forgiving one another and healing the long-standing hurts between families, so they felt united. The next time the government soldiers came, all two thousand people went to the village square. They made a big circle with their bodies and said to the soldiers, "We are one people, and if you want to take any of us, you will have to take us all." The soldiers left and never returned, and that village became one of the safest in Guatemala.

Another piece of this story is that most of the Guatemalan soldiers were teenage boys who were forced into the army, where they were brutalized and taught to kill. When they came back to their villages and realized what they had done, they were often suicidal. In Andrea's village, the people took what they had learned about forgiveness and offered it to these boys. They said, "We understand why you did what you did. You are still part of us. We love you and we want you to live."

Our experience in Guatemala not only motivated us to learn Spanish, but it also encouraged us to work in other countries that had experienced political violence, such as Argentina, South Africa, Nicaragua, and Northern Ireland. As in Guatemala, we saw that such violence is often rooted in unhealed hurts.

For example, we gave a conference to about two thousand people in Buenos Aires. This was after the end of the military dictatorship, in which people who opposed the government were arrested and often disappeared forever. I (Sheila) was introducing a presentation about healing grief. I was trying to relate to the people and what they had been through, so I began by saying, *"Ustedes han perdido a 30,000 desaparecidos"* ("You've lost thirty thousand people who disappeared.") Someone on one side of the auditorium yelled out in Spanish, *"No one* disappeared — that's all propaganda from Amnesty International!" (I found out later that the families of some of the generals were sitting there.) Someone on the other side of the room yelled back, "It's *not* propaganda, and there were sixty thousand *desaparecidos!"* And then everybody started yelling, as if they were fighting all over again.

I did not know what to do, and then the right words came to me as a free gift from I did not know where. I said, "Everyone here, on *both* sides, has suffered and lost loved ones. We want to focus on healing the grief you have all experienced." The room quieted right down, and I was able to lead them in a process for healing.

I had stumbled on a basic principle of nonviolence, which is that there are no enemies. There are only human beings with the same needs as ourselves, and part of nonviolent action is to want the best for everyone involved. We saw this when we gave retreats to Protestants and Catholics in Northern Ireland, to blacks and whites in South Africa, and to Contra and Sandinista families in Nicaragua. In every case, once the people realized that the enemy was not each other but rather the violence and grief of war, they were able to forgive one another and to heal.

Our experience has led us to believe that violence comes from hurts, and creates more hurt. We also believe that human beings can find nonviolent ways of resolving conflict, without all the suffering that violence brings. In what follows, we will demonstrate that nonviolent action has a long history and has proven itself to be far more effective than violence in even the most brutal situations (including against the Nazis), and that the capacity for nonviolence is innate and can be fostered through parenting, education, and a positive social environment.

Why Now?

Since the 2016 presidential election in the United States, the news has been full of stories of an increase in violence toward women, African Americans, Hispanics, Native Americans, Muslims, the LGBT community, and other minority groups. Swastikas are being painted on walls, bullying and racist attacks have increased, and schoolgirls are being sexually assaulted by schoolboys who cite the new president to justify their behavior.[2] These stories of violence and cruelty indicate simmering hurts, tensions, and frustrations in a large portion of our population that will likely take many years to heal.

At the same time, an even larger portion of our population is actively saying, "No more! Enough is enough!" Four of the five largest protest marches in American history have taken place in the last two years: the 2017 March for Science, the 2017 and 2018 Women's Marches, and the 2018 March for Our Lives.[3]

During this time period, one out of five Americans has participated in political rallies or protested in the streets, 19 percent of whom said they had never before attended a political gathering or joined a march.[4] Marching requires a high level of motivation:

> In some instances, marchers had to overcome serious limits on mobility to join. . . . For example, five people marched in the cancer ward at a Los Angeles–area hospital. Fifty women marched in a retirement community in Encinitas,

California. And 415 women's mobility was so limited that they participated in the women's march online.

Braving harsh weather was another test of intense motivation. In Alaska, 2,000 people marched in Fairbanks with a high temperature of 19 below zero; in Unalakleet, 38 or 40 people marched despite a windchill of 40 below. One woman in a Western mountain state was snowed in and couldn't get to the nearby town where she intended to march. Instead of giving up, she held a march of one in her own town.[5]

Because marching requires such a high degree of motivation, recent activism appears likely to translate into sustained political engagement and less demanding activities, such as voting. Typically, about 40 percent of eligible voters do not vote. But 83 percent of protesters and rally-goers say they definitely will vote, and nearly four in ten said they plan to become more involved in political causes in the future.[6]

Gloria Eive, who was the San Francisco chair of the Women for Peace march against the Vietnam War in 1965, says, "'All of the important achievements of the last 100 years have started with marches and protests.' A century ago, suffragists marched to win women's right to vote. Fifty years ago, protesters pushed for civil rights and an end to the Vietnam War."[7] Today, galvanizing issues include gun violence and climate change.

"We Are the Mass Shooting Generation"

At this moment, a group of high school students are among the most recognizable and vocal voices for change. On February 14, 2018, a gunman with an AR-15 assault rifle killed seventeen students and adults at Marjorie Stoneman Douglas High School in Parkland, Florida. This was one more in a long and heartbreaking history of mass shootings in the United States, in which more than 187,000 students from 193 primary or secondary schools have experienced a shooting incident during regular school hours.[8] As student Edna Lizbeth Chavez said, "I learned to duck bullets before I learned to read."[9]

But this time, the surviving Parkland students cried "Never Again!" and meant it. As eleventh-grader Cameron Kasky said, "We are the mass shooting generation."[10] He and his friends have had it. Although most of them cannot vote, make a hotel reservation, order a beer, or pay for a pizza without pooling their allowance, the Parkland kids have started a mass movement, which they call #NeverAgain.[11]

Parkland student reporters have used the skills they learned in journalism class and tech-savvy kids have used electronic media to spread their message. For example, as David Hogg hid from the gunman in a closet with other students, he used his cell phone to film and interview his classmates to document the attack. David said, "If I was going to die, I wanted to die doing what I love, and that's storytelling."[12] Senior Emma Gonzalez did not have a Twitter account before the shooting; eleven days later her followers outnumbered those of the NRA, and four weeks after that she had 1.2 million followers.[13] Articulate leaders such as Cameron, David, Emma, Jaclyn Corin, Alex Wind, and others were suddenly on all the major news programs.

In less than five weeks, the students organized protests and marches, including the seventeen minute March 14 school walkouts, in which three thousand schools participated, and the March 24 March for Our Lives, attended by 1.2 million people in the United States, as well as many others around the world. It was the largest youth-led and organized protest since the Vietnam War era. The mass-shooting generation, kids who have lived through enough active-shooter drills to know what it means to live in fear of gun violence, used the demonstration to expand voter registration. They encouraged supporters to do what some of them are not yet old enough to do for themselves: vote only for candidates who will support effective gun regulation.

The students built on what the Women's Marches in 2017 and 2018 had accomplished, and learned from previous movements, such as Black Lives Matter, Occupy, and Native American–rights activists, to reach out to a wide variety of minority groups rather than bask in their white privilege. As one commentator observed, "Perhaps protests have included so many people in the past two years because—get ready for it—they've made inclusion a central operating principle."[14] These efforts at inclusion are not only in terms of minority groups but also in terms of a wide range of issues that are inextricably linked. As evidenced by the signs that marchers carried, many participants in the March for Our Lives connected the epidemic of mass shootings in schools to the whole spectrum of violence, including militarism, war, inadequate health care, poverty, social inequality, and destruction of the environment.

For example, Greta Thunberg, a sixteen-year-old Swedish environmental activist who was inspired by the Parkland students, has mobilized millions of her peers around the world to address climate change. Greta has been nominated for a Nobel Peace Prize (see Conclusion: Stories of Hope).[15]

This Book Is for Everyone

This book was written for everyone old enough to read it: adults, college students, and high school students. As we will describe, the Parkland students and their #NeverAgain movement, as well as Greta Thunberg and the environmental movement, stand in a long history of youth and student activism. During the last century, every major U.S. social movement has had teenagers on the front lines.[16] We included chapters on the Standing Rock water protectors and on two examples of successful nonviolent resistance to the Nazis because, in each case, teenagers had starring roles.

Students were also fundamental to ending the Vietnam War and to the civil rights movement. For example, U.S. Congressman John L. Lewis, now seventy-eight, was a student leader of the lunch counter sit-ins in Nashville and a Freedom Rider in the 1960s. He was almost killed when a police officer bashed in his skull as Lewis marched from Selma to Montgomery with Martin Luther King Jr. Lewis joined the Atlanta March for Our Lives in support of the Parkland students, who are inviting their generation to be part of a long tradition of active nonviolence.

The stories we will share are wonder-ful. As we will discuss more fully later, wonder and cruelty cannot coexist in the human psyche. We hope that, as you read this book, you will be as fascinated and filled with wonder as we are by the magical power of nonviolence. We also hope you will use that sense of wonder to help heal ourselves, our country, and our world.

Reflection Process

1. Close your eyes and put your feet flat on the floor. Breathe slowly and deeply. Place your hand on your heart and imagine that you are breathing in and out through your heart.

2. Who in your life has modeled justice, fairness, courage, and care for others? What did they say or do that impressed you most deeply? How do you think that person's example has influenced you and the direction of your life?

3. As you continue to breathe in and out through your heart, breathe into yourself the qualities you most admire in this person, and let them grow in your heart.

Reflection Questions

What touched me most in this chapter is . . .

When I reflect on this chapter in relation to my life, I feel . . .

I want . . .

The Most Active Force in the World

Nonviolence is the greatest and most active force in the world. One person who can express nonviolence in life exercises a force superior to all the forces of brutality. My optimism rests on my belief in the infinite possibilities of the individual to develop nonviolence. The more you develop it in your own being, the more infectious it becomes till it overwhelms your surroundings and by and by might oversweep the world.

Mohandas Gandhi[1]

For many people, "nonviolence" means passivity, being "nice," and refusing to stand up for oneself. It is, however, the most powerful human force on earth, and perhaps the most misunderstood. Nonviolence is not antiviolence or the absence of violence; rather, it is a positive energy. Mohandas Gandhi, the foremost teacher of nonviolence in the twentieth century, described it as "the greatest force mankind has been endowed with."[2]

For Gandhi, disciplined, active nonviolence was a way of life encompassed by the Sanskrit word *satyagraha*. It includes the renunciation of physical force, but it is much more than that.[3] Gandhi liked to call it "love in action."[4] It is "positive action for true human good using only means that help and do not harm."[5]

As a positive force, nonviolence requires great courage and self-discipline. Gandhi emphasized that nonviolence is not for cowards, and he said it was better to fight than to be a coward because, "One had to be capable of violence before one could renounce it."[6]

Our misunderstanding of nonviolence as weakness or passivity has many sources. In Western culture, for non-Christians as well as Christians, one source of this misunderstanding is Jesus's exhortation to "turn the other cheek": "But if anyone strikes you on the right cheek, turn to them the left as well" (Matthew 5:38–42). In fact, according to our friend and mentor, theologian Walter Wink (see the Prologue), this passage means the opposite of how we have normally interpreted it. It is actually Jesus's teaching of nonviolent resistance, a "third way" between passivity and violence.[7]

The context of the passage is an everyday situation, typical of the oppressive, hierarchical society in which Jesus's followers lived as slaves of the Romans. In this situation, a less powerful person (such as a slave, a Jew, a wife, or a child) is being struck by a more powerful person (such as a master, a Roman, a husband, or a parent).

Why does Jesus specify being struck on the right cheek? He does so because, in his culture, the left hand was considered unclean, so only the right hand could be used to strike another. In order to strike someone on the right cheek with the right hand, one would have to backhand that person. In Jesus's culture, hitting someone with the back of the hand was a gesture of humiliation. The message was, "Remember your place . . . beneath me!"

If the oppressed person does as Jesus says and turns the other cheek—the left cheek—the only way the oppressor can strike that person with the right hand is with the front of the hand or with a fist. This was a gesture used only between *equals*. The message to the oppressor is, "I am not beneath you, I am your equal." Thus, the oppressed person has reclaimed his or her sense of dignity, without the use of violence. The other parts of the passage, regarding giving away one's undergarment and going the extra mile, have similarly surprising meanings and are actually also examples of nonviolent resistance to systemic humiliation and violence.[8]

Therefore, this passage actually demonstrates the first principle of nonviolence according to Gandhi, "that of non-cooperation with everything humiliating."[9] Michael Nagler, a scholar of nonviolence, believes that the founding moment of satyagraha was in 1906, when Indians in South Africa, led by Gandhi, took an oath not to obey any legislation that would deprive them of their human dignity.[10]

"Turning the Other Cheek" and Resisting Apartheid

When friends of ours returned from a trip to South Africa, they told us how often they had heard that Walter Wink's interpretation of turning the other cheek was instrumental in the relatively nonviolent end of apartheid (the system of racial segregation that had separated blacks and whites). Early in the struggle against apartheid, some groups in South Africa used violence to resist apartheid, but that only led to more violence. The churches did not want to get involved in violence, but they did not know what else to do. They were teaching their people to "turn the other cheek," which they thought meant only the refusal to strike back when they were mistreated.

Then Walter Wink, his wife, June, and their church community addressed 3,100 plain brown wrappers to the English-speaking clergy of South Africa. The wrappers disguised enclosed copies of a small book containing Walter's explanation of what it really means to turn the other cheek. The South African Roman Catholic Church sent out eight hundred more copies to its clergy. Thanks to Walter's book, the churches realized that they *could* do something.

Recalling what happened, Walter Wink writes, "What was previously understood as nonresistance and passivity, unfortunately thanks to the white missionaries, turned into . . . action, and did so by appeal to Jesus's own teaching."[11] The churches began to organize boycotts and other forms of nonviolent action that paralyzed the white businesses. They were successful in that their actions contributed to the end of apartheid. Recalling the impact of "the book in the plain brown wrapper" on the struggle to end apartheid, Methodist Bishop of South Africa Peter Storey later wrote, "South Africa is free now, liberated not by armed battalions but by millions of ordinary people refusing to collaborate any longer in their own oppression, and doing so largely nonviolently."[12] We might compare this to the Parkland students' refusal to settle any longer for politicians' messages of "thoughts and prayers" after every school shooting, and instead to demand real change in the form of effective antigun legislation.

In the case of South Africa, the most visible symbol of the end of apartheid was Nelson Mandela's release from prison and his election as president. Behind the scenes, however, was a long process of negotiation, in which Mandela (still locked up on Robben Island) met with the white regime:

> Mandela was both firm and flexible: Black South Africans, he insisted, would settle for nothing less than majority rule, but the end of white domination would not mean black supremacy, and whites would find a secure place in a democratic South Africa.[13]

Mandela intuitively understood Jesus's third way and that active nonviolence is based on the fundamental dignity and goodness of all human beings and wanting the best for everyone. As Martin Luther King Jr. put it, "Nonviolence does not seek to defeat or humiliate, but to win an opponent's friendship and understanding."[14]

Thus, for example, Gandhi knew that it was not good for anyone for the British to dominate India when India wanted to be free. Nevertheless, he did not treat the British as an enemy. He said, "We don't want to defeat the British. We want them to leave India as our friends."[15] Violence dehumanizes everyone involved, whereas nonviolence helps everyone recover their humanity. It reminds us that we are all brothers and sisters.

Reflection Process

1. Close your eyes and put your feet flat on the floor. Breathe slowly and deeply. Place your hand on your heart, and imagine that you are breathing in and out through your heart.

2. Recall a situation in which someone treated you unjustly or tried to humiliate you. Were you able to find a way to stand up for yourself without hitting back? How did you feel? What did you learn?

3. As you continue to breathe in and out through your heart, let the capacity to defend yourself without resorting to violence grow and deepen within you.

Reflection Questions

What touched me most in this chapter is . . .

When I reflect on this chapter in relation to my life, I feel . . . I want . . .

Chapter 1

The Two Hands of
Yes and No

Nonviolence gives us two hands upon the oppressor—
"one hand taking from him what is not his due,
the other slowly calming him as we do this."

Barbara Deming[1]

As Gandhi, King, and Mandela understood, when we are in touch with our own humanity and see everyone as a brother or sister, we refuse to be either a victim or a victimizer. This is the real meaning of turning the other cheek. An image for it is what peace activist Barbara Deming called "the two hands of forgiveness."[2] The two hands are a way to care for both ourselves and the other in a situation of oppression. We might imagine one hand extended with the palm facing outward, as if to say, "No! Stop! I will not allow you to mistreat me." The other hand reaches out to the oppressor and says, "Yes, I care about you, too, and I want the best for you."

We need both hands in every relationship. In relationships of love and trust, we usually use the hand that reaches out and maybe only occasionally do we need to put up the hand that says "No. Stop!" In relationships of abuse, oppression, or injustice, we need more of the hand that says no. But if we want to stop the cycle of violence, even in abusive relationships, we need to somehow find a way to use the other hand, as well—the one that reaches out and says, "Yes, I care about you, too." For example, Nelson Mandela did this when he reached out to include white South Africans in his black majority-rule government.

Similarly, in the Philippines, the people stood in front of the tanks on EDSA Boulevard and said to the soldiers with their hands (and their bodies), "No, we will not cooperate with President Marcos's attempt to steal our election." At the same time, they reached out to the soldiers with gifts of food and flowers to say, "We extend our love and care to you."

In the Guatemalan village where we first saw the power of active nonviolence, the people used the hand that says no to tell the returning soldiers, "We will not cooperate with what the military is trying to do to us." At the same time, they extended the other hand to them by saying, "We forgive you. You belong to us, and we do not want you to kill yourselves."

The two hands were equally effective when a robber crashed a dinner party. A group of friends were celebrating together, sharing wine and cheese on the patio before dinner. Suddenly a man with a gun appeared. He held the gun to the head of one guest and then another. At first, all the guests were paralyzed with fear. Then, one woman who refused to be intimidated said to the robber, "We're here celebrating. Why don't you have a glass of wine and sit down?" In effect, she put up one hand and said, "No, I will not participate in fear and violence." Using the other hand, she reached out to him with kindness. All of a sudden, the look on the man's face changed. He put the gun in his pocket, sat down, and drank a glass of wine.

After a little while, he asked, "Can I get a hug?" One guest hugged him, and then another. The man asked, "Can we have a group hug?" They all gathered around and embraced him. The robber said he was sorry and left, taking his glass with him. The group of friends, still shaken but relieved, ate dinner. As they opened the front door of the house to leave, they saw the empty glass, unbroken and neatly placed on the sidewalk by their alley.[3]

Another story of the two hands comes from the civil rights movement. A group of black students who were peacefully demonstrating in Montgomery had been tricked by police into dispersing and then beaten. The police would not allow ambulances to reach the wounded students for two hours. The driver of one of those ambulances drove to Selma and told a crowd of black and white activists what had just happened.

> The crowd ... seethed with rage. Cries went up: "Let's march!" Behind us, across the street, stood, rank on rank, the Alabama State Troopers and the local police forces of Sheriff Jim Clark, itching for a fight. The situation was explosive. A young black minister stepped to the microphone and said, "It's time we sang a song." He opened with the line, "Do you love Martin King?" "Certainly, Lord!" the crowd responded. "Do you love Martin King?" "Certainly, Lord!" "Do you love Martin King?" "Certainly, certainly, certainly, Lord!" Without warning he sang out, "Do you love Jim Clark?" "The sheriff?! Cer- certainly, Lord," came the stunned, halting reply. "Do you love Jim Clark?" "Certainly, Lord." It was stronger this time. "Do you love Jim Clark?" "Certainly, certainly, certainly, Lord."
>
> The Reverend James Bevel then took the mike. We are not just fighting for our rights, he explained, but for the good of the whole society. "It's not enough to defeat Jim Clark—do you hear me, Jim?—we want you converted. We cannot win by hating our oppressors. We have to love them into changing."[4]

James Bevel and the crowd were determined to resist Sheriff Jim Clark and his forces but they were equally determined to reach out to them with love.

James Bevel understood how to use the two hands to lead the crowd in responding to an oppressor. With one hand, he said to the sheriff, "No more hate." With the other hand, he said, "We have the power of love, and we love you, too."

Resisting Nazis with Humor
and the Two Hands

The civil rights movement was a response to white supremacy. Unfortunately, we are still dealing with it fifty years later. We write this about two years after a white supremacist, neo-Nazi gathering in Charlottesville, Virginia, in which many people were injured and a woman protesting the gathering was killed. More such gatherings are being planned in other cities. How can the two hands be used in these situations to prevent more violence?

Commenting on the white supremacist gathering in Charlottesville, nonviolence scholar Dr. Maria Stephan says, "I would want to punch a Nazi in the nose. . . . But there's a difference between a therapeutic and strategic response . . . violence is simply bad strategy."[5] A therapeutic response uses the hand that reaches out to understand the opponent's anger, aggression, and underlying wounds, and avoid exacerbating those wounds with more anger and aggression. One way to do this with white supremacists is through humor.

The residents of Wunsiedel, a small town in Germany, used the two hands to make fun of Nazis. Because Rudolf Hess, Hitler's deputy, was buried there, for twenty-five years Wunsiedel has been the site of an annual neo-Nazi march. In an effort to stop it, the residents tried counterdemonstrations, as well as exhuming Hess's body and removing his gravestone. However, the annual march continued.

The people of Wunsiedel felt helpless until, in 2014, they began a campaign now known as "Nazis against Nazis." Local businesses and residents pledged 10 euros (about $12.50) for every meter the Nazis marched, to be donated to EXIT Deutschland, a program that helps people leave neo-Nazi and other extremist groups.[6] The townspeople turned the march into "Germany's most involuntary charity walk" and a parody of a sporting event. A starting line, a halfway mark, and a finish line were stenciled onto the street. Brightly colored posters with slogans such as, "If only the Führer knew!" were displayed along the route. A sign reading "Mein Mampf!" ("My Munch," a takeoff on Hitler's book, *Mein Kampf*) was hung over a table of free bananas for the marchers. Pink banners were hung around town, thanking the "dear Nazis" for their donation. At the end of the route, the townspeople cheered the neo-Nazi marchers on to the finish line. The marchers were showered with confetti, offered certificates of completion, and greeted by a sign thanking them for contributing about 10,000 euros to EXIT Deutschland and the anti-Nazi cause.

The following year, only about half as many Nazi marchers showed up in Wunsiedel. They no longer hung around or gave out information. Other towns in Germany and one in Sweden have used similar tactics against neo-Nazis, with similar results. Several American groups are now trying to organize people to resist white supremacists by imitating the people of Wunsiedel and turning white supremacist rallies into opportunities to raise money for antiracist causes.[7]

The Wunsiedel villagers used the two hands in the form of humor. With one hand, they said to the neo-Nazis, "We won't allow you to spread fear and hatred in our town." With the other, they said, "This is not good for you, and we will use your march to fund your recovery, whenever you are ready."

Well-chosen humor is a powerful strategy because it avoids escalation, reveals the absurdity of positions based on hatred and racism, and deflates the puffery of insecure people who try to appear strong by bullying others. Violence, on the other hand, is bad strategy because,

> Violence directed at white nationalists only fuels their narrative of victimhood—of a hounded, soon-to-be minority who can't exercise their rights to free speech without getting pummeled. It also probably helps them recruit. And more broadly, if violence against minorities is what you find repugnant in neo-Nazi rhetoric, then "you are using the very force you're trying to overcome."[8]

Moreover, according to Dr. Stephan, oppressive regimes and movements foment violence because "violence and discord help their cause. So why would you do what the oppressor wants you to do?"[9]

When we use the two hands, we remind both our opponent and ourselves that violence is not the greatest force we have. The greatest force and the most effective strategy, as Jim Bevel understood, is love. This is true because humans intuitively know that we are all one and that harm to any of us is harm to all of us.

Greg Boyle, who has worked with gang members in Los Angeles for many years and gained their trust, refers to this as a sense of "kinship." He writes that if we focus on kinship, justice will come naturally.[10] The two hands are an expression of our kinship with all people and our insistence that every person is of equal value and must be treated with love and respect.

Reflection Process

1. Close your eyes and put your feet flat on the floor. Breathe slowly and deeply. Place your hand on your heart and imagine that you are breathing in and out through your heart.

2. Think of a person in your life with whom you do not feel safe. How far out do you need to put the hand that says, "No, I will not allow you to mistreat me"? How far out do you want to put the other hand that says, "I care about you, too"? Play with the positioning of your hands until they feel exactly right for your relationship with this person. Now think of a person with whom you feel very safe. Position your hands in a way that matches your experience of this relationship. Again, adjust them until they feel exactly right.

3. As you continue to breathe in and out through your heart, breathe into yourself the ability to balance yes and no in every relationship.

Reflection Questions

What touched me most in this chapter is . . .

When I reflect on this chapter in relation to my life, I feel . . .

I want . . .

Chapter 2

Nonviolence in Ordinary and Extraordinary Times

*With kinship as the goal, other essential things fall into place
. . . were kinship our goal, we would no longer be promoting
justice—we would be celebrating it.*

Greg Boyle[1]

The power of *satyagraha*, or love in action, can be effective in
every situation of potential violence, from bullying among children, to a Nazi death camp, to ethnic conflicts. For example, a
young boy used nonviolence to escape from a bully:

> This boy was the smallest in his class, and he had chronic
> sinusitis. His nose was always running. On his school bus
> there was a bully who was terrorizing everyone. Finally,
> one day the little kid had had it. Blowing a load of snot into
> his right hand, he approached the bully, his hand out. "I
> want to shake the hand of a real bully," he said. The bully
> backed up until he reached the back of the bus, where he
> sat down and never bothered anyone again. That nose was
> always at the ready![2]

The small boy used his nose to care for both himself and the
bully. The boy refused to allow himself to be a victim, and he
refused to allow the bully to be a victimizer.

Another victim of bullying, Natalie Hampton, had physical scars as a result, but even worse were her memories of the isolation she endured in middle school when she had to eat lunch alone every day. Although she switched to a new school where she had a group of supportive friends, she had not forgotten what it was like to be an outcast. "'Whenever I saw someone eating alone, I would ask that person to join our table, because I knew exactly how they felt. I saw the look of relief wash over their faces,'" she said. Natalie decided to create a new app that she called "Sit with Us." The app allows students to make it known that they will welcome anyone at their lunch table, and other students can check this list of "open lunches" and sit down at a lunch table with no chance of rejection. Those who decide to be Sit-with-Us ambassadors pledge to welcome anyone to their lunch table and include them in the conversation.[3]

I (Sheila) wish I had known a Sit with Us ambassador when I was in school. I was extremely shy, and I was bullied for reasons that really had nothing to do with me, although I did not understand that until I was an adult. I'm not a naturally aggressive person, and I would not hit back. I did not know how to use the hand that says, "No. Stop it!," and I did not have a community of caring people to support me, except for one boy whom I will never forget.

When I was in sixth grade, I went to a new school. I had no friends, and other children ridiculed me. On Valentine's Day, the others exchanged cards, but I was nobody's Valentine and everyone knew it. I somehow managed to get out of my classroom unnoticed and went to the playground. I sat alone on a swing, utterly bereft. I did not notice him coming, but a boy from my class sat down on the swing next to mine. His name was Richard, and he wore glasses. He began to swing alongside me. I don't remember if he said anything, only that he was with me, and I was not alone any more. Richard had friends, but he chose to live from a sense of kinship with someone who didn't and to be in solidarity with me.[4]

Solidarity

Solidarity with the oppressed is a basic principle of active non-violence, and it is the heart of Sit with Us. Natalie's app gave more socially comfortable students a way to be in solidarity with those who had fewer social skills and less confidence. Solidarity means a refusal to let anyone be separated out and victimized. What happened in Guatemala was like bullying on a large scale, to the extent of genocide. It was solidarity that protected the people in Andrea's village, symbolized by the circle they formed to convey to the soldiers, "We are one people, and if you want to take any of us, you will have to take us all."

The Overland High School girls soccer team in Denver, Colorado, understood this. When a Muslim teammate was prohibited by the referees from playing in a game because of her hijab, all her non-Muslim teammates wore hijabs for the game as well.[5]

Christians in Billings, Montana, also understood solidarity. When the Schnitzer family prepared their home to celebrate the Jewish holiday of Chanukah by putting a menorah in five-year-old Isaac's window, a neo-Nazi hate group shattered the window with a cinderblock. The next morning the FBI advised Tammie Schnitzer to remove all signs of Chanukah from her home. But Tammie was not willing to back down in the face of terrorism. She called the *Billings Gazette* to report what had happened.

The next day, the executive director of the Montana Association of Churches read about the attack and put a menorah up in her own window, as a sign of solidarity with the Schnitzers. The idea spread. The Billings Coalition for Human Rights began running off pictures of menorahs for all the people who wanted to support their Jewish neighbors. Dry cleaners and convenience stores gave out paper menorahs; one store called for more after they went through five hundred copies in one day. The *Billings Gazette* published a full-page color menorah and encouraged its fifty-thousand subscribers to hang it in their windows. Schoolchildren hung menorahs in their classroom windows for passersby to see.

On the eighth and last night of Chanukah, Tammie and Brian Schnitzer drove their children around Billings. Menorahs were everywhere. Isaac said, "I didn't know so many people were Jewish." His mother answered, "They're not all Jewish. But they're our friends."[6]

An Israeli restaurant owner is an equal opportunity "solidizer."[7] He understands the power of food to remind people of their common humanity, and he gives a 50-percent discount to any table where Arabs and Jews sit together. He told the *Times of Israel*, "By us we don't have Arabs! But we also don't have Jews. . . . By us we've got human beings! And real excellent Arab hummus. And great Jewish falafel!!"[8]

When white supremacists planned their gathering in Charlottesville, Virginia, they tried to rent Airbnb houses to sleep and have parties. As one participant wrote, "We've taken over all of the large Airbnbs in a particular area. . . . We've set up 'Nazi Uber' and the 'Hate Van' to help in moving our people. . . ." Through such messages, Airbnb members became aware that white supremacists had booked listings. These members notified Airbnb, whose policy is to ask all members to commit themselves to "our mission of belonging" and to "accept people regardless of their race, religion, national origin, ethnicity, disability, sex, gender identity, sexual orientation, or age." Because white supremacy is antithetical to this commitment, Airbnb responded to the bookings by deactivating the accounts of those hosting the white supremacists, as well as those of the renters. Airbnb stands in solidarity with all human beings, especially the most vulnerable, and will not cooperate with racism and hatred.[9]

The Parkland students' #NeverAgain movement, which was itself born out of solidarity with anyone who has suffered violence, has in turn inspired many expressions of solidarity. For example, the students led a nationwide seventeen-minute school walkout one month after the mass shooting at their school, to commemorate the loss of seventeen students and adults. While many school administrations were supportive, others threatened punishment, such as suspensions. In one case, three high school students who participated in the walk-out chose to be paddled with a wooden bat instead of suspension, so they would not miss class or eligibility for team sports.[10] In response to threats of punishment, numerous college admissions officials expressed solidarity with students by tweeting their support and assuring prospective applicants that walking out would not jeopardize their college admissions. For example, Worcester Polytechnic Institute (WPI) wrote,

> HS [high school] students are worried that getting suspended for peacefully protesting against gun violence may hurt chances to get into college. Not @ WPI. WPI believes students should hold fast to their values & principles. We review our applicants with an eye towards who they are as people.[11]

Choosing to Nonviolently Offer Our Life for Others

Although surprisingly few people die through nonviolent action,[12] sometimes the death of one willing person can save the lives of many. For example, during World War II, a Polish prisoner escaped from Auschwitz. The standard punishment for such an event was to force the hundreds of other prisoners in the same cell block to stand at attention until the escapee was found. If he or she was not found, ten of the others would be put in an underground cell without food or water, where they would starve to death.

In this case, the escaped prisoner was not found, and ten other prisoners were chosen to die. Then another man, Maximilian Kolbe, stepped forward. He had no children, and he asked to take the place of one of the condemned men, who was a husband and father. News of this example of love in action spread through the camp and gave the prisoners the will to live:

It was an enormous shock to the whole camp. We became aware someone unknown among us in this spiritual night . . . was raising the standard of love on high. Someone unknown, like everyone else, . . . went to a horrible death for the sake of someone not even related to him. Therefore it is not true, we cried, that humanity is cast down and trampled in the mud. . . . Thousands of prisoners were convinced the true world continued to exist and that our torturers would not be able to destroy it. . . . To say that Father Kolbe died for one of us or that person's family is too great a simplification. His death was the salvation of thousands.[13]

Although Kolbe died (by his own choice), he nonviolently saved perhaps thousands of others, including Franciszek Gajowniczek, the husband and father whose place he took, who died only recently at the age of ninety-three.[14] Kolbe's willingness to be in solidarity with a condemned man, even to the point of death, illustrates the power of nonviolence to remind us that we are all in it together.

The same nonviolent sense of solidarity saved the lives of many children in Rwanda during the genocidal violence between Hutus and Tutsis in 1994:

In Rwanda a tribal militia, bent on genocide, herded children out of their school and ordered them to separate themselves into Hutus and Tutsis. The children knew what it meant. They refused. The soldiers yelled at them, but the children were undaunted. The soldiers gave up and went away. Amid all that slaughter, when the value of life had all but disappeared, the mere willingness of some schoolchildren to suffer for justice [stopped] a blood-crazed band of soldiers. . . .[15]

This story illustrates the power of nonviolence to work in even the most desperate situations and to humanize even the most vicious opponents. Although our culture is convinced that we

must resort to violence to defeat opponents, especially brutal
ones, the history of nonviolent resistance and recent research
demonstrate otherwise.

Reflection Process

1. Close your eyes and put your feet flat on the floor. Breathe
slowly and deeply. Place your hand on your heart and imagine
that you are breathing in and out through your heart.
2. Recall a moment when you stood up for a person or group
of people you cared about. How did you find the courage you
needed? What did you say or do? How did you feel in the midst
of the situation, and how did you feel when it was over?
3. As you continue to breathe in and out through your heart,
breathe into yourself the courage you had in this situation, and
let it grow within you.

Reflection Questions

What touched me most in this chapter is . . .
When I reflect on this chapter in relation to my life, I feel . . .
I want . . .

Chapter 3

Surprising New Evidence for the Power of Active Nonviolence

You say you want a revolution? Then leave the guns behind. . . .
Nonviolent resistance can be a near-unstoppable force for change
in the world, even in the most unlikely circumstances.
                              Erica Chenoweth and Maria Stephan[1]

Dr. Erica Chenoweth was a doctoral student in political science at the University of Colorado in Boulder. She was studying the use of violence to create political change, and her approach was based on her mainstream belief that violence is tragic but necessary. Then she received an invitation to an academic workshop on nonviolent resistance in Colorado Springs. The organizers were intentionally reaching out to traditional scholars such as Erica, in hopes that they would teach about nonviolence in their classes. Erica accepted the invitation, in part because, "It came with free books!"

At the conference, participants shared stories of the successful use of active nonviolence. Erica countered every story with one about how nonviolence had failed and/or how violence had succeeded. As Erica tells it, "You can imagine how unpopular I was!" Finally, Maria Stephan, one of the conference organizers, said to Erica in so many words, "If you are so certain that nonviolence doesn't work as well as violence, I dare you to prove it." Erica took the dare.[2]

Erica and Maria, who became her research partner and coauthor, were the first to list, analyze, and compare all 323 known cases of major violent and nonviolent campaigns for the overthrow of a government or for territorial liberation, with more than one thousand participants, from 1900 to 2006.[3] In their book *Why Civil Resistance Works,* they concluded that nonviolent campaigns were twice as likely to succeed as violent ones, 54 percent of the time versus 26 percent of the time, in terms of accomplishing the goals of the campaign. (See Appendix, Chart 1 and Fig. 1.)

Moreover, nonviolent campaigns were ten times more likely than violent ones to result in democracy within five years. Democratic governments followed violent campaigns successfully only 5 percent of the time, and civil war within ten years was 15 percent more likely than in nonviolent campaigns.[4] The success rate of nonviolent campaigns increased over time, so that during the fifty years prior to 2010, nonviolent campaigns became increasingly successful and common, whereas violent campaigns became increasingly unsuccessful and rare.[5] (See Appendix, Fig. 2.)

Although nonviolent campaigns are still more common and more effective than violent ones, from 2010 to 2016 there was a drop in the effectiveness of nonviolent campaigns. Erica Chenoweth attributes this primarily to their success. She writes: "Nonviolent mass movements are the primary challengers to governments today."[6]

Precisely because this form of resistance has been so successful, repressive regimes recognize the threat to their power posed by nonviolent campaigns. They have studied the strategy and tactics of nonviolence, and they have become more "politically savvy" in their use of "smart" repression. This is not a reason to lose confidence in active nonviolence. Rather, it makes it all the more important that people committed to active nonviolence stay ahead of the game by becoming even *more* politically savvy than their opponents, in ways we will describe in future chapters.[7]

According to Chenoweth and Stephan, the key to the success of nonviolent campaigns is mass participation. They built on earlier research that found that any campaign in which more than 5 percent of the population is involved will be successful, and they discovered that the figure is actually lower. In every case where at least 3.5 percent of the population was involved, the campaign was successful. The only campaigns that reached that level of participation were nonviolent ones.[8]

More people will participate in nonviolent campaigns because the barriers to participation are lower than for violent ones. For example, people who cannot or do not want to take the physical risks involved in violence, such as the elderly, women, children, or handicapped people, can participate in nonviolent campaigns. Also, in a nonviolent campaign everyone can have access to information; they can know what action is planned and when it is happening, unlike in clandestine military activities. The level of commitment in terms of time, energy, and degree of risk required in nonviolent campaigns is much less than in violent ones, so people can go on with their daily lives. Finally, people who have a moral resistance to killing will be far more willing to participate in a nonviolent campaign than a violent one. For all these reasons, nonviolent campaigns attract much greater participation.[9]

An example is the 1986 People Power Revolution in the Philippines:

> From metropolitan Manila and the surrounding provinces, upwards of two million people poured into the streets. Like the "armies" of Gandhi and King, there were young and old, women and men, whole families. The wealthy, the middle class and the poor were there. They stayed, day after day and through the nights, singing, praying, and talking. A remarkable spirit prevailed. There were no pickpockets and no crimes. People shared food and water,

while others opened their homes to strangers for the use
of toilets and a place to rest.[10]

When large numbers of people are involved, as they were in
the Philippines, they have a wide range of skills to contribute to
the campaign. They are also more likely to have connections to
a significant number of those who support the existing regime,
such as security forces, economic elites, state media, religious
authorities, and so on, and these people will then be more open
to reevaluating their support for the regime.

Regime loyalists will have friends and family among a large
group of nonviolent resisters, and this will affect their reaction.
For instance, in Serbia, when Slobodan Milošević was overthrown in 2000, police officers started to disobey orders to shoot
demonstrators. When one officer was asked why he would not
shoot, he said, "I knew my kids would be in the crowd."[11]

As with Serbian police officers, other authorities, such as religious leaders, can play an important role in nonviolent action.
In the Philippines, religious leaders were prominent supporters
of the revolution. For example, Cardinal Jaime Sin of Manila
was seen as the "field marshal . . . of the unarmed forces of the
Philippines."[12] The soldiers loyal to Marcos were greatly influenced in their decision to defect by the courage and nonviolent
faith of religious leaders.[13]

Another reason nonviolent campaigns involving mass participation are more successful is that if regime forces do react
violently and attack unarmed people, the backlash is usually
very great. This leads to even more resistance to the regime, as
well as pressure from the international community.[14] A violent
reaction on the part of regime forces actually increases the likeli-
hood that a nonviolent campaign will succeed. Chenoweth and
Stephan found that when there is a violent crackdown, if the
nonviolent campaign continues to rely on nonviolent strategy,
the probability of the campaign's success increases by about 22
percent.[15] For those who are committed to nonviolent action,

part of being "politically savvy" is resisting the temptation to violence in the face of a violent crackdown.

However, if any violence is used by a nonviolent campaign, including the destruction of property, the chances of success are diminished. Chenoweth suggests that the decrease in the effectiveness of nonviolent campaigns beginning in 2010 may be in part because, as these campaigns have become more popular, they include a higher number of participants who are not well trained and who lack the discipline to resist all temptations to violence.[16]

In contrast, although the Philippine People Power Revolution involved millions of people, they had been well trained and were able to remain nonviolent. When Filipino opposition leader Benigno (Ninoy) Aquino returned to the Philippines after three years in the United States, he was murdered by government forces as he descended from an airplane in Manila. The Marcos-controlled press did not report Aquino's death. Only Radio Veritas, a local Roman Catholic radio station, announced it. Nevertheless, the news spread, and two million people peacefully lined EDSA Boulevard for Aquino's funeral procession. This motivated even more resistance to the Marcos government from the Filipino people, disrupted the Marcos government's relationship with the United States, and gained the sympathy of the world.[17]

Chenoweth and Stephan found that nonviolence can succeed even in brutal, repressive contexts, as it did in the Philippines. In fact, all 323 cases they studied were highly repressive situations. Their findings contradict the myth that nonviolence worked against the British in India because they were "fair minded," but that it would never have worked against the Nazis.[18] In fact, British colonial rule was often brutal and ruthless.[19] Moreover, according to Chenoweth and Stephan, active nonviolence can and did work against genocidal dictators such as Adolf Hitler and Joseph Stalin.

One example involving the Nazis is the 1943 Rosenstrasse protests in Berlin, where Aryan German women obtained the release of their Jewish husbands who had been imprisoned by the Nazis.[20] Other examples are from Bulgaria, Finland, Norway, and Italy, where most or all Jews were saved by nonmilitary resistance.[21] In this book, we will focus on the rescue of the Danish Jews (see chapter 8) and the French village of Le Chambon-sur-Lignon, where five thousand villagers saved five thousand Jews (see chapter 9). Unfortunately, true nonviolent resistance was not often used against the Nazis. What was mostly used was passivity,[22] and when violent resistance from within a country they invaded was used against them, it failed.[23]

Chenoweth and Stephan conclude,

> Insurgents who claim that violent resistance is necessary are probably always wrong. . . . Many of the groups that claim violence as a last resort may have never attempted strategic nonviolent action, judging it to be too difficult at the outset. . . . [However,] nonviolent resistance has the potential to succeed in nearly all situations in which violent resistance is typically used, and to more favorable ends in the longer term. . . . Nonviolent resistance can be a near-unstoppable force for change in the world, even in the most unlikely circumstances.[24]

The success of active nonviolence is good news in a world wracked by war and violence. Approximately 75 million people were killed in wars during the twentieth and twenty-first centuries.[25] In comparison, relatively very few people have been killed during nonviolent resistance campaigns compared to violent ones.[26]

Moreover, as all great religions teach, and as Chenoweth's and Stephan's research demonstrates, "violence always begets violence . . . all violence blows back!!"[27] For example, the death penalty does not deter homicide but actually seems to increase it by about 2 percent, because the underlying message is that human life is expendable.[28] The widespread availability of guns in the United States correlates with a higher rate of gun violence than in countries where gun ownership is limited. And war is an endless cycle. Violence is, as Martin Luther King Jr. said, "a descending spiral begetting the very thing it seeks to destroy. Instead of diminishing evil it multiplies it. . . . Hate cannot drive out hate; only love can do that."[29]

Reason for Hope

Despite the drop in the effectiveness of nonviolent campaigns from 2010 to 2016, we may now be seeing their resurgence. As we mentioned in the Prologue, four of the five largest protest marches in American history took place during the last two years, 2017 and 2018, and 19 percent of participants had never before joined a march or attended a protest gathering.

Chenoweth guesses that 1.3 percent of the U.S. population was involved in the Women's March, and she notes that "U.S. conditions are ripe for more women's—and other—protests in the coming years."[30] Besides making use of technological resources, such as Facebook and Twitter, to network and alert participants, activists are learning from recent experiences. Chenoweth writes,

> There's a lot of increased capacity for organizing because of the experiences of the past ten years. . . . Black Lives Matter itself gave young people a lesson on how you do this. Before Black Lives Matter there was Occupy, since then we've had the Dreamers, the Women's March, and Muslim Ban protests in airports. . . . My guess is these kids did their first activism with their moms. It's a quicker learning curve for kids.[31]

Recall that Erica Chenoweth and Maria Stephan found that if 3.5 percent of the population participates in a campaign, it will be successful. We may not be far from that critical point of 3.5 percent.

Reflection Process

1. Close your eyes and put your feet flat on the floor. Breathe slowly and deeply. Place your hand on your heart and imagine that you are breathing in and out through your heart.

2. What social issue matters most to you at this time? What experience in your life causes you to care about this issue? How far would you be willing to go to work for change? For example, would you vote accordingly, dialogue with someone who thinks differently, sign a petition, join a protest march, risk being arrested?

3. As you continue to breathe in and out through your heart, breathe into yourself the qualities you need to take action on this issue, and let it grow within you.

Reflection Questions

What touched me most in this chapter is . . .

When I reflect on this chapter in relation to my life, I feel . . .
I want . . .

Chapter 4

Nonviolence Has Been Working Like Crazy

In just the last few years, nonviolence has emerged in a way that no one ever dreamed it could emerge in this world. In 1989 alone, there were 13 nations that underwent nonviolent revolutions. . . . That year 1.7 billion people were engaged in national nonviolent revolutions. That is a third of humanity. If you throw in all of the other nonviolent revolutions in all the other nations in the 20th century, you get the astonishing figure of 3.34 billion people involved in nonviolent revolutions. That is two-thirds of the human race. No one can ever again say that nonviolence doesn't work. It has been working like crazy.

Walter Wink[1]

Active nonviolent accomplishments of the twentieth century include Danish resistance to the Nazis during World War II in places such as Denmark, Bulgaria, Italy, Norway, and Le Chambon, France; Indian independence from the British in 1947, under the leadership of Gandhi; the American civil rights movement in the 1960s; the People Power Revolution in the Philippines in 1986; the overthrow of the dictator Augusto Pinochet in Chile in 1988; the rise of Solidarity and the end of Communism in Poland in 1989; the fall of the Communist regime in East Germany, Hungary, Bulgaria, and Mongolia in 1989; the end of apartheid in South Africa in 1994; and the end of Slobodan Milošević's regime in Serbia in 2000. Although in some of these situations there were occasional outbreaks of violence on the part of individuals or small groups, ultimately success came through active nonviolence.[2]

As Walter Wink says in the quote above, in 1989 alone, 1.7 billion people were involved in nonviolent revolutions. Two million of them were organized by the Popular Front for Latvia, to resist Soviet rule. On August 23, 1989, they formed the longest unbroken human chain in history, stretching 420 miles across two rivers and connecting the capitals of Latvia, Estonia, and Lithuania. They were successful, and in 1990, Latvians regained control of their government.[3]

As mentioned in chapter 3, during the past fifty years nonviolent campaigns have, overall, become increasingly successful and common, whereas violent campaigns are becoming increasingly unsuccessful and rare. Studies of active nonviolence attribute an increase in success rates during the last years of the twentieth century in part to the mass media. The U.S. civil rights movement in the 1960s, the People Power Revolution in 1986, and the rise of Solidarity in Poland in the 1980s were all broadcast around the world on television. These successful movements encouraged other nonviolent movements to believe they, too, could be successful. Also, Richard Attenborough's 1982 movie *Gandhi* inspired the leaders of the Philippine People Power Revolution and of nonviolent resistance to Pinochet in Chile.[4]

Active Nonviolence throughout History

The great success of nonviolent action in the twentieth century is built on a long history of thousands of years. All major ancient religions included nonviolence as an ideal. For example, the Buddhist emperor Ashoka, who ruled in Northern India from 273 to 232 B.C.E., renounced violence as an instrument of conquest.[5]

In Western history, the foundation of nonviolence is the teachings of Jesus. In his view of Jewish law, weapons, military, and war were illegal. Christianity was based on love, which was seen as incompatible with killing: "The early Christians are the earliest known group that renounced warfare in all its forms and rejected all of its institutions."[6] Although the Romans tried to force Christians into the military, for three centuries most of them refused; they were "Western history's 'first conscientious objectors.'"[7] Islam, too, had a tradition of nonviolence, as reflected in the following passage from the Quran: "whoever kills a human being should be looked upon as though he had killed all of mankind."[8]

When Christianity became the official state religion under Constantine in A.D. 312, war and serving in the military became more acceptable to Christians, although some still refused military service. Over time, with the development of the "just war" theory by Augustine of Hippo in the fifth century, whereby killing for "godly" reasons was justified, and then the Crusades beginning in the eleventh century, the Catholic Church endorsed violence. In Islam, as well, the tradition of nonviolence was overcome to some degree by the needs of the state. For example, the word *jihad* originally meant striving for godly perfection, but as Muslims got involved in wars, *jihad* came to mean striving to win militarily.[9]

In Christianity, during the Middle Ages, the monastic movement was a way that Christians could still reject warfare, and there were always Christian groups in Europe who were nonviolent, such as the Waldensians (late 12th century), the Anabaptists (16th century), and the Mennonites (16th century).[10] The Quakers, founded in England by George Fox in the 17th century, were one of the foremost groups advocating nonviolence. Quaker William Penn's "holy experiment" in nonviolence in Pennsylvania, beginning in 1782, worked for more than 70 years. Penn treated Native Americans with kindness and respect, and tried to prevent their exploitation by Europeans.[11]

During the American Revolution, eighty-thousand Americans belonged to nonviolent groups who were opposed to war. This was more than the number of soldiers that George Washington ever had under his command at any point during the Revolutionary War.[12] Many nonviolent methods of resisting the British were used in the colonies during the Revolutionary period, including writing pamphlets, a boycott of British goods, such as cloth, and the Boston Tea Party.[13]

Some scholars believe that these nonviolent methods of resistance alone would have been sufficient to gain independence from the British, and violence would never have been necessary. They suggest that the war was fought for economic reasons rather than for reasons of liberation.[14]

By the early nineteenth century, there were various peace organizations in the United States, which united into the American Peace Society in 1828.[15] Arguments for nonviolence joined with arguments for the abolition of slavery, led by William Lloyd Garrison. From 1831 to 1866, he published *The Liberator*, a newspaper that promoted nonviolent abolitionism and was widely influential.[16] Meanwhile, Harriet Tubman ran the Underground Railroad, a nonviolent way to help slaves escape from their masters. There were war resisters on both sides during the Civil War.[17]

One of the most influential war resisters of the nineteenth century was Henry David Thoreau, who refused to pay taxes because of his opposition to slavery and the Mexican-American War. His 1849 essay "Civil Disobedience" would later have a great influence on Gandhi and Martin Luther King Jr.[18] The successful women's suffrage movement, from the mid-1800s until the passage of the Nineteenth Amendment in 1920, was also committed to nonviolence.

Across the globe, in New Zealand, in the late 1800s, the Maori leader Te Whiti led a successful nonviolent campaign to preserve his people's land from settlers who tried to take it.[19] In the late nineteenth and early twentieth centuries, peace organizations formed in many countries, and international peace conferences were held. Unfortunately, World War I took place anyway, but many thousands of war resisters refused to serve. Also, one of the most famous stories of spontaneous nonviolent resistance took place during World War I, the Christmas Truce of 1914.

The Christmas Truce

On the first Christmas Eve of World War I, British, French, and German troops were stationed in Belgium and France, along either side of "No Man's Land," an area about two football fields wide that marked the battle line. This true story has several versions, depending on the memories of who is recounting it. One version is that Germans began to sing "Stille Nacht," the German version of "Silent Night," and British troops sang back in English. Then the Germans improvised what looked like Christmas lights. Soon a brave soldier from one side walked toward the other, holding a white flag. Instead of shooting him, someone from the other side went to meet him. Before long, their comrades had come up out of the trenches.

The two sides embraced one another, exchanged gifts, shared photos from home, played soccer, and sang together. Approximately 100,000 soldiers participated in the Christmas Truce. It spread along about two-thirds, or four hundred miles, of the front line and lasted around two weeks. The truce ended only when officers threatened to court-martial soldiers who fraternized with the enemy (a crime punishable by death in wartime, presumably because putting a human face on "the enemy" makes it difficult if not impossible to kill them).[20]

As we were completing this book, we visited the site of the truce near Ypres, Belgium, near the French border. We saw a lot of battlefields, military cemeteries, and statues of generals during that trip. But in the region of Ypres are memorials to the miracle of love and peace that happened there. Even the soccer field has been preserved, with a reconstructed trench on either side of an open, grassy area, and a mound of soccer balls donated by visitors from all over the world.

Back in the United States

Opposition to war continued through World War II, when conscientious objectors constituted one out of every six inmates in U.S. federal prison.[21] Nonviolent resistance was used during that war, and it was successful even against the Nazis in several instances, when it was actually tried (see chapters 8 and 9). More recently, nonviolent action has been used to protest wars, such as those in Vietnam, Iraq, and Afghanistan.

During the war in Vietnam, there were massive and repeated peace demonstrations at home in the United States and abroad. In the military itself, according to Pentagon documents, there were over 500,000 incidents of desertion by American soldiers who had become war resisters.[22] Unlike the Christmas Truce of 1914, resistance on the ground in Vietnam and fraternization with the "enemy" were so widespread that military commanders could not control or stop it. In the end, this resistance contributed to ending the war.[23]

Active nonviolence has also been used on behalf of a vast array of social causes besides ending the war in Vietnam, including women's suffrage, civil rights, LGBTQ rights, higher wages and fair conditions for workers, and boycotts of foods containing GMOs. Recently, football player Colin Kaepernick led a movement to kneel down or "take a knee" during the singing of the national anthem at sports events to protest racism. He chose the national anthem, "The Star Spangled Banner," because the third stanza celebrates the death of black slaves who fought for the British during the War of 1812.[24] His teammates, the San Francisco 49ers, responded by giving him an award for courage, the Len Eshmont Award, named after a Navy veteran who was an original member of the team and exemplified "inspirational and courageous play."[25]

Gandhi

During the past century of this long history of nonviolence, the two most influential figures have been Mohandas Gandhi and Martin Luther King Jr. Gandhi was born in India in 1869. He went to South Africa as a young lawyer in 1893. The turning point in his life came when a white conductor threw him off a train because he sat in the first-class section, reserved for whites. The following day, he began organizing the Indian community in South Africa to resist segregation, and he continued there for the next twenty years. During this time, Gandhi studied Thoreau, corresponded with Leo Tolstoy (who was committed to nonviolence), and developed the concept of *satyagraha*.

In 1914, after negotiating a settlement with the South African government on behalf of the Indian community, Gandhi returned to India. Back in his homeland, he traveled widely, listened to the poor, and studied how he could apply what he had learned about *satyagraha* in South Africa to India's struggle for independence from the British.[26]

For the rest of his life, as the Indian people and eventually the whole world watched, Gandhi devoted himself to "the first widespread application of nonviolence as *the* most powerful tool for positive social change."[27] He pointed out that there were 100,000 British soldiers controlling 350 million Indians and said, "We must not hate the British. They have not taken our government from us. We have given it to them."[28] He encouraged the Indian people to take it back.

Gandhi's most famous campaign was the Salt March to the Sea in 1930, in which he led his followers 240 miles to the coast to gather salt water and to make salt illegally, in protest of British taxes on salt and British law forbidding Indians to make their own. Subsequently, Gandhi organized a raid on the Dharasana salt works, where the violent reaction of British soldiers and the nonviolent response of the Indian people was broadcast around the world.[29] As Chenoweth and Stephan point out, the violence of the British only gained more sympathy and support for Gandhi and his followers.

Ultimately Gandhi was successful, and India was granted independence on August 14, 1947. However, to Gandhi's dismay, violence erupted between Hindus and Muslims, and Gandhi was assassinated by a Hindu fanatic on January 30, 1948.[30]

According to the Dalai Lama,

> Mahatma Gandhi's great achievement was to revise and implement the ancient Indian concept of nonviolence in modern times, not only in politics, but also in day-to-day life. Another important aspect of his legacy is that he won independence for India simply by telling the truth. His practice of nonviolence depended wholly on the power of truth.[31]

When we visited Gandhi's ashram, Sabarmati, in Ahmedabad during a recent trip to India, what moved us most was this devotion to truth in all its simplicity and purity. In Gandhi's room, we did not see any statues or altars—only his desk and spinning wheel. We walked past a room where he invited an untouchable family to live as full members of the community, an act so contrary to Hindu custom that Gandhi's own sister left the ashram in protest. We saw the dirt around trees covered with grains of flour that ashram members had left as food for the ants, and we watched squirrels and wild birds moving freely among the visitors without fear. We bought a copy of Gandhi's autobiography in the bookstore for U.S. $1.20 . . . hardly a way to make a profit from tourists. Gandhi's ashram, now celebrating its one hundredth anniversary, is a living witness to his apprehension of and commitment to the truth of our kinship with all humans and all other creatures.

Martin Luther King Jr.

Gandhi's work was one of the primary influences on Martin Luther King Jr. King did not initially believe in nonviolence, but he did care about injustice. When he was very young, he worked in a factory that employed both blacks and whites. He saw that poor whites were as exploited as blacks, and he realized the problem was not white people but rather a system of exploitation.[32] Then, as a student at Morehouse College, King read Thoreau's essay "Civil Disobedience." "Fascinated by the idea of refusing to cooperate with an evil system, I was so deeply moved that I reread the work several times."[33] While attending Crozer Seminary beginning in 1948, he went to a talk on the teachings of Gandhi. The "message was so profound that I left the meeting and bought a half-dozen books on Gandhi's life and works."[34]

King studied Gandhi's campaign of active nonviolence, and he was greatly impressed by the concept of *satyagraha* and Gandhi's leadership of the Salt March to the Sea to protest British control of salt in India. King wrote,

> Gandhi was probably the first person in history to lift the love ethic of Jesus above mere interaction between individuals to a powerful and effective social force on a large scale. Love for Gandhi was a potent instrument for social and collective transformation. It was in this Gandhian emphasis on love and nonviolence that I discovered the method for social reform that I had been seeking for so many months.[35]

When King finished his seminary training in 1953, he went to Montgomery, Alabama, to pastor a church. He did not go with the intention of starting a nonviolent campaign. Rather, as events unfolded, King saw Gandhi's method of nonviolent resistance as the most powerful option for helping his people lift themselves out of oppression: "Living through the actual experience of the protest, nonviolence became more than a method to which I gave intellectual assent; it became a commitment to a way of life." Many of King's remaining questions about nonviolence "were now solved in the sphere of practical action."[36]

Dr. King became the focal figure in the movement to end racial segregation during the 1960s that culminated in the Civil Rights Act of 1964. Children, teenagers, and young adults were critical to this movement. Students integrated lunch counters, rode buses as Freedom Riders, walked out of segregated schools, attended marches and rallies, and often endured prison. King's leadership of the American civil rights movement remains the primary example in U.S. history of active nonviolence. His nine-year-old granddaughter's presence at the March for Lives in Washington, DC, on March 24, 2018, is an acknowledgment that the current student movement is the grandchild of the civil rights movement.

King's life and work have inspired a vast array of organizations, scholarship, and movements. These include resistance to the Dakota Access Pipeline, which we will discuss in the following chapter.

Reflection Process

1. Close your eyes and put your feet flat on the floor. Breathe slowly and deeply. Place your hand on your heart and imagine that you are breathing in and out through your heart.

2. If you were in a seemingly impossible situation and you wanted to respond nonviolently, who would you want to help you find a solution? This could be one or more people you know, or one or more historical figures.

3. As you continue to breathe in and out through your heart, imagine that person or persons beside you, and breathe in what you need from them.

Reflection Questions

What touched me most in this chapter is . . .

When I reflect on this chapter in relation to my life, I feel . . .

I want . . .

Chapter 5

The Water Protectors

The water protectors at Standing Rock flipped the notion of what it means to be a courageous warrior. It is no longer about the capacity to inflict violence; being a warrior now means the courage to stand unarmed in the face of danger, to protect vulnerable people and places, and to be willing—as the veterans at Standing Rock said—to take a bullet to protect the sacred.[1]

A contemporary example of active nonviolence in the spirit of Dr. King's emphasis on love for the opponent is the Dakota Access Pipeline (DAPL) resistance, led by Native Americans who refer to themselves as "water protectors" (in contrast to the terms "protesters" or "demonstrators" often used by the media to describe them). The water protectors' choice of this name seems significant and consistent with their emphasis on unity; water and protection are life-affirming desires that all humans share, including ourselves who come from water-challenged Colorado.

While we were writing this book, the three of us took a break and went to the Standing Rock Sioux Reservation in North Dakota to join the water protectors and thousands of their supporters from all over the world in protecting the land and water of the Standing Rock Sioux from the proposed pipeline. We wanted to go in part because of our personal connections to the Sioux people. A member of the Sioux community serves on the board of directors for our non-profit organization. As a young Jesuit, I

(Denny) taught high school students on the Rosebud Sioux Reservation. As a high school junior, I (John) participated in a service project on the Pine Ridge Reservation, where I worked side by side with Sioux teenagers. All three of us have experienced the deplorable conditions in which these young people live on the reservation, and it was deeply moving to us that Native American teenagers started the pipeline demonstration.

On July 15, 2016, a group of about thirty Sioux teenagers, led by thirteen-year-olds Tokata Iron Eyes and Ann Lee Rain Yellowhammer, began a two-thousand-mile relay run from Standing Rock to Washington. They wanted to deliver a petition asking the Army Corps of Engineers to stop the pipeline. The teenagers were following a Lakota Sioux tradition, in which the tribe sent runners to communicate with Sioux groups in other regions. Along the way of the relay run, thousands of people joined the teenagers by running with them, following along in cars with food and water, and offering shelter.[2]

The runners arrived in Washington in early August, and they were granted a meeting with officials from the Department of the Interior. These officials then asked the Army Corps of Engineers to provide a full Environmental Impact Statement for the project. From this grew the movement by the water protectors and their supporters to stop the DAPL.[3]

Unity and Solidarity

The water protectors established a camp on Standing Rock land near Cannonball, North Dakota. Eventually the number of participants would average six thousand, sometimes growing to as many as eleven thousand.[4]

The first thing we saw as we entered the camp was hundreds of flags lining the beginning of the dirt road that circles the area—flags of all the tribes and other groups who are united in opposition to the pipeline, including those from other countries. Some of the American tribes represented by the flags had been at war for centuries, but now they were joined together in peaceful resistance to protect what they value in common.

The Native Americans at the camp understood that in order to maintain an attitude of peaceful resistance and unwavering commitment to nonviolence, in the face of extreme police brutality, they had to be one with each other. We met a white friend who was living at the camp as a volunteer, and she took us on a tour, where we met camp members who were sharing and caring for one another in every aspect of life.

Our friend showed us whole tents for the storage and preparation of food, most of it donated by supporters from all over the United States. We saw tents full of blankets and warm jackets for whoever needed them. We walked by people chopping wood for fires to keep their friends warm. We visited a medical tent, staffed by Veterans for Peace, where free traditional medical care was provided, and learned of another one offering free alternative medical care (massage, herbs, aromatherapy, etc.). Our friend also showed us the teepee that had been converted to a school, where she was teaching children.

She and other white volunteers are examples of widespread solidarity with the water protectors. Another example is what happened when law enforcement began collecting names from Facebook of people who signed in as being at the camp. Around this time, Denny's sister told us that her daughter was there. It turned out that she was only virtually there . . . she was one of at least 1.5 million people from around the world who signed in on Facebook as being at the camp. They did this as a way to protect camp members by confusing law enforcement as to who was actually there, and as a sign of solidarity with the water protectors.

Love for the Opponent

Gandhi and Martin Luther King Jr. emphasized love for one's opponent. The water protectors' unity and care for one another helped them to demonstrate this. For example, we attended the daily morning prayer service, where the people gathered in a circle around the sacred fire. A Native American woman prayed for the police and emphasized that they were not the opponent; the opponent is the system that oppresses everyone.

Representatives of that system, including a group of six hundred clergy and a group of four thousand veterans, came to the camp to demonstrate their solidarity with the Native American people and to apologize for the role of the church and the military in the long and terrible history of atrocities committed against Native Americans.[5] A prayer service at which a leader of the veterans knelt down and asked forgiveness from a leader of the water protectors was broadcast around the world.[6]

Our favorite story of love for the opponent at Standing Rock is when the Morton County, North Dakota, sheriff's department ordered the water protectors to evacuate their camp, claiming that the people would not have enough food and adequate shelter to sustain themselves through the harsh winter. The sheriff's department also put out a list of needed supplies for the police (who are working on behalf of the oil company), such as hand warmers and energy bars. The Morton County officers had exhausted their $10 million budget and were asking the white community for donations. The Native American water protectors saw the list and brought the police what they needed, saying, "We have enough to share. Generosity is an original teaching for the Lakota."[7]

Failure or Success?

The water protectors' resistance to the DAPL can look like a failure because the pipeline was completed, and oil is flowing through it. However, it may actually be one of the great successes of nonviolent action. We see three ongoing effects of the water protectors' active nonviolence:

First, more than 380 tribes from all over the world, including New Zealand's Maori and the Ecuadorian Kichwa, joined the water protectors. One of their leaders said, "That's a very significant time in history: when the tribes come together collectively and unite and say, Enough is enough."[8] Millions of supporters worldwide donated money, signed petitions, divested from oil-related investments, and marched in their own cities and towns. The pipeline resistance has unleashed the courageous warrior energy of many who are "willing to take a bullet to protect the sacred."[9]

Second, the water protectors' resistance to the pipeline, centered in tiny Cannonball, North Dakota—a place that is difficult to even find on a map—has contributed to a worldwide environmental movement. For example, the pipeline protest helped encourage some large banks to divest from oil companies.[10] When Donald Trump proclaimed that the United States would drop out of the Paris Climate Accords, other countries, as well as some American states and cities, vowed to fulfill the commitments of the accords anyway, inspired at least to some extent by the water protectors.

Third, the water protectors have given us a lesson in walking in the shoes of the oppressed. When my family joined the demonstration at Standing Rock, I (Denny) realized that my son John was now the same age I was when, as a student, I lived and worked for two weeks with the Sioux on the Rosebud Reservation. At that time I experienced the same hospitality and warm welcome my family received at Standing Rock, as well as the oppression that tried to grind the native people down every day of their lives.

As an eighteen-year-old, the welcome I received was shocking to me. After all, I had grown up like many white kids, playing cowboys and Indians. I and all my playmates were always, of course, the good guys, shooting and killing the imaginary Indians (none of us wanted to *be* an Indian) from the safety of our tent. There I was, as an eighteen-year-old, welcomed into the Sioux's wind-blown shacks and offered their only chair as I sat down to eat dinner with Indians whom I had imagined killing by the hundreds! After living with them for only a few days, in the blowing sand and sweltering heat of the reservation, in shacks that had no running water, I understood how we "good guys" had oppressed them. Those days formed friendships that changed the course of my life. I committed myself to acknowledge when I am an oppressor and to walk in the shoes of the oppressed. Thus, I returned to the reservation three years later to teach in their school.

The water protectors gave the whole world an opportunity to experience what I did. They taught us all what it means to be oppressed, and how we "good guys" participate in their oppression. The three of us wonder how many of those who watched the story of Standing Rock unfold, whether from afar or by actually visiting the camp, had their lives permanently changed, as my life was changed when I went to the Rosebud Reservation. As we mentioned in the Prologue, waves of activism have spread across this country during the past two years. We suspect that many of those waves are coming from Standing Rock.

The unleashing of collective warrior energy, the growth of a worldwide environmental movement, and a lesson in oppression are only three examples of the ongoing effect of the DAPL resistance. Nonviolent action is sometimes a mysterious process, in which we plant seeds that grow to fruition only slowly and gradually. It may be a long time before we see the full impact of a movement that began with a few Native American kids who ran two thousand miles for the sake of their people's land and water.

Reflection Process

1. Close your eyes and put your feet flat on the floor. Breathe slowly and deeply. Place your hand on your heart and imagine that you are breathing in and out through your heart.

2. When have you been with a person or a group of people who experience oppression in a way that you have not experienced it and who helped you understand this particular form of oppression? Did you become aware of any way in which you participate in their oppression?

3. As you continue to breathe in and out through your heart, breathe into yourself the capacity to be in solidarity with those who are oppressed, and let it grow within you.

Reflection Questions

What touched me most in this chapter is . . .

When I reflect on this chapter in relation to my life, I feel . . . I want . . .

Chapter 6

Outsmarting the Powers

There is no such thing as objective powerlessness. Our belief that we are powerless is a sure sign that we have been duped by the Powers.

Walter Wink[1]

As soon as we arrived at the main camp of the DAPL resistance at Standing Rock, we were invited to attend active nonviolence training. The facilitator, a Native American man, had clearly spent years in nonviolence training himself, and knew how the basic strategy and tactics could be applied to the specific situation of resisting the pipeline (see chapter 11).

The Standing Rock resistance community is following in the tradition of the American civil rights movement. For example, Martin Luther King Jr. would not allow anyone to participate in a nonviolent direct action unless he or she had attended training. This training included simulated violent attacks by white segregationists and practice in not reacting to insults and protecting oneself from severe injury without striking back, such as by covering one's head or rolling into a ball.[2]

Similarly, the People Power Revolution in the Philippines may have appeared to be a spontaneous response to the murder of Benigno Aquino and Marcos's theft of an election. However, in fact, hundreds of thousands of Filipinos in communities all over the country were trained in nonviolence for years prior to the moment when it was clearly time to put all that training into action. Since fair elections are one means of active nonviolence, 500,000 Filipinos were trained by the Catholic Church to monitor elections.[3]

Strategy and Tactics of Active Nonviolence

So, what are the strategy and tactics of active nonviolence? They are something of a science in and of themselves, and they have been carefully studied and developed during the past century. Much of this work was done by Gene Sharp, who is regarded as "the great theoretician of nonviolent power."[4]

Sharp's basic theory is that problems of oppression exist because one group that seemingly has more power appears to have the ability to impose its will on a group that seemingly has less power. The members of the seemingly weaker group do not believe they could ever have enough power to change this situation. As Walter Wink puts it, they have been duped by the oppressor into believing they are powerless. Change can come only when oppressed people understand that the power of oppressors is dependent on the support and cooperation of the people, and that the people can withdraw their cooperation.[5]

Gandhi understood this very well. He knew that in order to free themselves from oppression, the Indian people needed to recognize that they had allowed the British to take over their country, and that they had the power to withdraw their cooperation and obedience. He saw this as an interior movement away from passivity and submission toward courage and self-respect. Much of Gandhi's effort was to help his people recover their self-respect, often in the most basic ways.

For instance, the Indian people were wearing clothes made from imported British cloth. Gandhi encouraged them to return to their ancient tradition of spinning cotton and weaving the cloth (known as "khadi") for their clothes, rather than disempowering themselves by allowing the British to take over something so fundamental to their dignity as their clothing.[6]

Currently, the Parkland students are following Gandhi by refusing to accept that they are powerless in the face of the NRA. They insist that laws *can* be passed that will help stop gun violence and that lawmakers who refuse to do this will be voted out of office.

The Six Sources of Power

According to Sharp, once people own their power to stop their oppression, the sources of the oppressor's power need to be identified so that the most vulnerable ones can be undermined. They include the following:[7]

1. *Authority*. Whatever oppressors use to assert their own power or legitimacy, especially the people's belief that the oppressor's rule is legitimate and that their moral duty is to obey it. For example, praising "law and order" is often code for telling people that they should obey the government, the police, the military, and so forth. Religion is often used to enforce authority by presenting political leaders as chosen and blessed by "God."

2. *Human Resources*. The people who support or prop up the ruler or leader. They may be members of the same ethnic or political group, such as the white police who enforced segregation in the American South. Or, it may be local people who have been persuaded to support a foreign occupier. In India, there were many local Indian officials, known as "headmen," who worked for the British and encouraged the Indian people to obey British laws.[8]

3. *Skills and Knowledge*. Needed by the regime to carry out its agenda and supplied by those who cooperate with the ruler or leader. A modern example might be people who collect electronic data regarding those who have or might challenge the oppressor. In the case of the DAPL resistance, supporters confused this data collection by law enforcement officials

who worked for the oil companies by signing in on Facebook as if they were at the Standing Rock camp.

4. *Attitudes or Beliefs*. About obedience, patriotism, and so forth that may encourage people to assist and obey the ruler or leader. For example, the response of most Americans to the national anthem is to obediently stand, put their right hand over their heart, and start singing. When Colin Kaepernick "took a knee" (kneeled down rather than stood) during the "Star Spangled Banner," he was undermining this reflexive, patriotic response.

5. *Material Resources*. The extent to which the oppressor has access to or controls property, natural resources, the economy, transportation, means of communication, and so forth. Gandhi disrupted British control over India's natural resources and economy by encouraging Indians to make their own salt rather than pay the British salt tax and weave their own cloth rather than buy British cloth.

6. *Sanctions*. Ways of enforcing cooperation by threatening or applying punishment, such as imprisonment or execution, to those who are disobedient. An example would be the use by law enforcement of pepper spray, plastic bullets, and water hoses in freezing weather on nonviolent protesters at Standing Rock.

The goal of nonviolent action is to disrupt these sources of power, as the water protectors did by linking arms and nonviolently standing their ground at Standing Rock, while journalists documented police brutality. An example mentioned earlier of disrupting human resources that we find especially moving is the Serbian police officer who would not shoot into a crowd of demonstrators because he knew his children would be there. One reason Chenoweth and Stephan emphasize the importance of mass participation in nonviolent action is that when large numbers of people withdraw their cooperation, they can more effectively disrupt more sources of power than can small numbers of people.

Three Basic Ways of Disrupting
the Six Sources of Power

Disrupting any of the six sources of power can be done in three basic ways: protest and persuasion, noncooperation, and inter-vention.[9] The first and mildest is *protest and persuasion*, which makes it clear that some of the population is opposed to the policies of the ruler or leader. Methods of protest might include leaflets, marches, petitions, and protest meetings. Examples are the March on Washington in 1963, which drew the world's attention to the American civil rights movement; the Women's March in 2017, which demonstrated the depth of opposition to the policies of the incoming presidential administration; and the 2018 March for Our Lives, which encouraged Americans to end gun violence.

The second method of disrupting the sources of power is noncooperation, such as strikes and boycotts. This can weaken the opponent's power, control, and wealth, and can even pro-duce paralysis. An example is the grape boycott begun in 1965, led by Cesar Chavez on behalf of California farm workers to secure better wages and working conditions. This paralyzed the grape growers, and in 1970 the workers won a collective bar-gaining agreement.

A recent example is when Parkland student leader David Hogg call for a boycott of Laura Ingraham's Fox News program. Laura had sent a Tweet ridiculing David because he was not accepted into all of the colleges to which he applied. David ral-lied his 600,000 Twitter followers and asked them to urge her advertisers to withdraw their ads from her TV and radio shows. Within about two weeks, twenty-six advertisers had stopped their ads. Laura apologized to David, who said he would accept her apology "only if you denounce the way your network has treated my friends and me in this fight. It's time to love thy neighbor, not mudsling at children." During a subsequent interview, he added, "If she really wants to do something, she could cover inner-city violence and the real issues that we have in America."[10]

The third method of disrupting the sources of power is *intervention*, which disrupts the established order and threatens the opponent's control. This can include sit-ins, occupation (such as parks or other gathering places), and overloading facilities such as prisons. This happened when African American students sat at segregated lunch counters in Nashville during the civil rights movement. This disrupted business at the lunch counters. Moreover, as one group was arrested, another took their place until the Nashville jails could not hold any more prisoners. The students refused bail, and the system was overwhelmed.[11]

Within the three basic methods of nonviolent action are hundreds of possible specific actions. Gene Sharp emphasizes the importance of long-term strategic planning for nonviolent campaigns, which means using the best actions and methods for the situation at hand and knowing you have the needed resources available to be successful.[12]

Strategic Planning . . . and Universal Love

Gandhi and King understood Sharp's basic contention that oppressors have power only so long as the oppressed give it to them by cooperating, and this cooperation can be withdrawn. They also understood Sharp's emphasis on strategic planning, choice of the best method to disrupt the sources of the oppressor's power, and having the needed resources. For example, Gandhi chose to focus on resisting the unjust British salt laws, because salt was a basic human need with which every Indian could identify, and large numbers of Indian people were willing to join Gandhi in the salt campaign. Resisting the salt laws would disrupt an important British material source of wealth and power. Having the needed resources available includes having participants who are prepared. Thus, as mentioned earlier, Martin Luther King would not allow anyone to join a nonviolent direct action unless that person had been through a training workshop, and the DAPL resistance in North Dakota followed King's example in this regard.[13]

However, whereas Sharp emphasized using active nonviolence for practical reasons, because it works better than violence, Gandhi and King began from a foundation of love and ultimate truth. They both believed the universe is founded on love and that nonviolence is consistent with love, whereas violence is not. They used nonviolent strategy brilliantly, before Gene Sharp articulated it, but they believed that what really gives nonviolence its power is the energy of love, which Gandhi and King saw as the fundamental energy of the universe.

King believed that we are all connected as kin. On some level we know that what happens to other human beings in some way happens to us, too, so that,

> no man can continue to debase or abuse another human being without eventually feeling in himself at least some dull answering hurt and stir of shame. Therefore . . . when an oppressor's violence is met with forgiving love, he can be vitally touched, and even, at least momentarily, reborn as a human being, while the society witnessing such a confrontation will be quickened in conscience toward compassion and justice.[14]

King's belief that we are all connected in this way underlies his "Six Principles of Nonviolence,"[15] in which he emphasizes the goodness in everyone and the importance of love for the opponent as well as for oneself:

1. Nonviolent resistance is not a method for cowards; it does resist.
2. Nonviolence does not seek to defeat or humiliate the opponent, but to win his friendship and understanding.
3. Nonviolence is directed against forces of evil rather than against persons who happen to be doing the evil.

4. Nonviolent resistance is a willingness to accept suffering without retaliation, to accept blows from the opponent without striking back.

5. Nonviolence avoids not only external physical violence but also internal violence of spirit. The nonviolent resister not only refuses to shoot his opponent, but he also refuses to hate him.

6. Nonviolent resistance is based on the conviction that the universe is on the side of justice.

King's assumption of the connectedness and innate goodness of human beings is exemplified by the Children's March in Birmingham in 1963, protesting school segregation. The children faced commissioner of public safety Bull Connor, an adamant segregationist, and his forces:

Thousands of children marched through the streets right up to the firemen. In the days before, many were brutalized when those fire hoses were turned on them. But the youth learned the lessons of Dr. King. "Nonviolent suffering love is always redemptive," he said in every talk. "We will match your capacity to inflict suffering with our capacity to accept suffering and we will wear you down until justice comes."

So they came back, asking for more. Bull Connor went ballistic. "Turn on those hoses," he screamed at the firemen. The marchers knelt in prayer. "We're not turning back," they said. They stood up and walked right toward the firemen.

"It was one of the most fantastic events of the Birmingham story," King later said. "I saw there, I felt there, for the first time, the pride and power of nonviolence."

While Bull Connor screamed and yelled, the white firemen and police officers were overcome by the singing youth. The firemen couldn't bring themselves to hurt the kids again. So they put down the fire hoses. Some of them started crying. The singing youth walked right through them.[16]

Reflection Process

1. Close your eyes and put your feet flat on the floor. Breathe slowly and deeply. Place your hand on your heart and imagine that you are breathing in and out through your heart.

2. Think of a situation in which you feel oppressed and powerless. Notice what happens in your body as you get in touch with this situation, and notice what emotions you feel. Straighten your body in a way that expresses your dignity and value, and observe any shift in your emotions. Now position your two hands, the one that says, "No, you cannot mistreat me," and the one that says, "I care about you, too." Adjust your hands until they are in the position that most helps you regain a sense of your own power.

3. As you continue to breathe in and out through your heart, pay attention to any ideas or images of ways that you could regain your power in this situation.

Reflection Questions

What touched me most in this chapter is . . .

When I reflect on this chapter in relation to my life, I feel . . . I want . . .

Chapter 7

Humanizing Ourselves and Our Opponent

The truth of the others' humanity is denied in all violence . . .
before you can bring yourself to kill others or injure them, you
have to reduce people to "enemies" or animals or, even better,
to objects.

Michael Nagler[1]

While Gene Sharp's strategy and tactics for nonviolent action
have proven their effectiveness, the actual practice of nonviolence, as Gandhi and King understood it, is based on the common humanity and goodness of every person. The beginning
of our ability to do this is to be at peace within ourselves, feel
good about ourselves, and know our own value.[2] Gandhi knew
this very well, and he emphasized that Indians could not drive
out the British until they had first "driven out . . . their own
demons."[3]

When we are at peace with ourselves and know our own
goodness, we are capable of the first principle of nonviolence,
which is the refusal to cooperate with anything that is humiliating. We don't act like victims, and we don't encourage others
to victimize us. The small boy with sinusitis may have disliked
himself because of his runny nose, but at some point he must
have decided that he deserved respect from the bully rather than
abuse, and the boy refused to be a victim anymore. In Sharp's

terms, the boy realized that he did not have to cooperate with an oppressor and found a way to withdraw his cooperation.

When we are in touch with our own goodness and the goodness of others, we can establish a relationship based on the two hands of forgiveness. The two hands are a way to humanize our opponent, and it is recognizing our common humanity that has the power to overcome violence. One way to humanize our opponent is to behave like a human being ourselves.

The water protectors did this when they offered hand warmers and energy bars to the Morton County police. Karen Ridd did this when she was working in El Salvador with Peace Brigades International, along with her friend Marcela, who is from Colombia. They were suddenly arrested by the Salvadoran National Guard. Before they were taken away, Karen, who is Canadian, had time to call the Canadian consul. The two women were taken to an army barracks, where they were blindfolded and interrogated. They could hear the sounds of torture and sobbing from victims in nearby rooms. Meanwhile, the Canadian government put pressure on the Salvadoran government to release Karen. A few hours later,

> Karen found herself walking across the barrack grounds toward a waiting embassy official . . . a free woman. But when the soldiers had removed her blindfold inside the barracks she had caught a glimpse of Marcela, face to the wall, a "perfect image of dehumanization." Glad as Karen was to be alive, something tugged at her. Feeling terrible, she made some excuses to the exasperated Canadian official who had come all the way from San Salvador to get her, turned, and *walked back into the barracks,* not knowing what would happen to her in there, but knowing it could not be worse than walking out on a friend.
>
> The soldiers were startled, and almost as exasperated. They handcuffed her again. In the next room, a soldier banged Marcela's head against the wall and said that some

"white bitch" was stupid enough to walk back in there, and "Now you're going to see the treatment a terrorist deserves!" ... But Karen's gesture was having a strange effect on the men. They talked to Karen, despite themselves, and she tried to explain why she had returned: "You know what it's like to be separated from a *compañero.*" That got to them. Shortly after, they released Karen and Marcela. The two women walked out together under the stars, hand in hand.[4]

Because Karen behaved like a human being, she brought out the deeply buried humanity of the soldiers and saved her own life and that of her friend.

Karen befriended her opponent. I (John) did this in a much less dangerous situation, when I was eight years old and participated in a peace demonstration in front of the White House. When I saw all the police officers guarding the area, I was afraid they would arrest me. I went up to a police officer and asked him, "What would I have to do to get arrested?" He smiled at me and answered, "I won't arrest you unless you cross over that fence onto the White House grounds." I said, "Okay, I won't do that." He smiled again, and I felt connected to him. Rather than treat my opponent as an enemy, I had done two things to humanize him: I made friends with him, and I let him know what I would and would not do, so he wouldn't be taken unawares. Gandhi did something similar when he planned the Salt March to the Sea: he made sure that the British knew exactly what he was going to do.

Violence Cannot Coexist with Wonder

Another way to humanize our opponent is by doing something surprising that causes a sense of wonder, as in the stories of the man who gave his pizza to two other men who were fighting and the group of friends who offered a robber a glass of wine (see chapter 1). Wonder creates what Angie O'Gorman calls a "context of conversion," because the human psyche cannot be in a state of both wonder and cruelty at the same time.[5]

For example, our Mexican friend, Tesha, was in a pharmacy in Mexico City. A man with a gun walked in, intending to rob the store and threatening to shoot anyone who resisted. Without thinking and in a firm voice, Tesha blurted out, "Our Lady of Guadalupe is watching you!" The robber appeared astonished that this slender, fragile-looking woman had spoken up to him. Tesha had used wonder to deter him from cruelty. Besides that, no Mexican man wants to upset Our Lady of Guadalupe. He dropped his gun and ran out of the store.

Gain Sympathy

Because we want the best for everyone, the practice of active nonviolence includes not trying to provoke an attack, since this would not be good for either our opponent or ourselves. However, if we are attacked, it is important to get as much sympathy from the rest of the world as possible, through maximum publicity. This puts more pressure on our opponents and withdraws whatever support they might have.

Thus, for example, Gandhi drew the world's attention to the Amritsar Massacre in 1919, in which British soldiers slaughtered 379 unarmed Indians, because it exposed the brutality of the British and gained sympathy for the Indian people.[6] During the American civil rights movement, televised scenes of black children being attacked by police dogs, and of peaceful marchers being clubbed and beaten by police, aroused the sympathy of Americans for the cause of civil rights.

In the case of the DAPL protest, whenever the police reacted violently to the water protectors, donations to the protest increased. One example is a supporter named Ho Waste Wakiya Wicasa, who set up a GoFundMe account, hoping to raise $5,000 for the water protectors. On Thursday of that week, 140 of them were evicted from the camp and arrested. These actions by the police made international news, and by Friday Ho Waste Wakiya Wicasa's account had raised more than $200,000. As police brutality continued and the water protectors remained nonviolent, donations to the account eventually grew to more than a million dollars.[7]

These examples support Chenoweth and Stephan's point that a nonviolent campaign is more likely to grow and succeed if regime forces react violently, so long as the campaign remains nonviolent.[8] We saw this the year after we participated in the annual demonstration to close the School of the Americas at Fort Benning. An elderly Jesuit friend of ours, Bill Brennan, who is in a wheelchair, attended the demonstration. Although he did not cross the line onto Fort Benning property, he was arrested. A photograph of Bill in police custody was broadcast around the world, arousing outrage that an elderly man in a wheelchair had been arrested for entirely nonviolent behavior. Such images are powerful ways to gain widespread sympathy for nonviolent action and put pressure on oppressors.

Agents Provocateurs

Because getting sympathy is so important, the practice of active nonviolence includes not allowing ourselves to be provoked into violence. Experienced practitioners of nonviolence are familiar with *agents provocateurs*. These are people planted by those in power. For example, they may be planted at a peace demonstration. The intention of *agents provocateurs* is to try to provoke violence by striking someone, throwing rocks, etc., in hopes of getting a violent reaction, which would destroy the effectiveness of the demonstration.

While at Standing Rock, we heard a report from the sheriff's office that a man was shot by one of the Native American water protectors closer to the actual pipeline construction site than ourselves, and many people were arrested. After we returned home and investigated the incident, it turned out that it was the supposed shooting victim who had actually fired shots. Documents found in the truck he was driving indicate that he was a security guard for the oil company, driving a company-owned truck.[9]

The incident generated a lot of confusion and stories in the mainstream news that implied violence on the part of the Native Americans. The shooter appears to have been an *agent provocateur,* whose purpose was to undermine public sympathy for the Native Americans' resistance to the Dakota Access Pipeline. The planting of *agents provocateurs* is so common that in a talk to Iraq War protesters in Boston, Howard Zinn called out the FBI agents in the crowd, saying, "We know you're here, and we won't allow you to provoke us into violence."[10]

In the case of the DAPL, besides the incident described above, the use of *agents provocateurs* was brought to a whole new level. Energy Transfer Partners, the company building the pipeline, hired TigerSwan, a private security company that had worked for the U.S. government as a military contractor in conflict zones such as Iraq. TigerSwan convinced the multiple law enforcement agencies gathered at the pipeline construction site that the water protectors were jihadist terrorists intent on blowing up the pipeline in order to justify an extensive military operation. Thus, police used many of the same military strategies and military grade equipment, including missile launchers, against the water protectors that TigerSwan had used in Iraq.[11]

All of this was designed to provoke the water protectors, whose intention was peaceful protest, into violence. This level of provocation to violence and the involvement of TigerSwan are consistent with Chenoweth's observation that governments are developing new strategies to try to defeat nonviolent movements.[12] Often, as in this case, government forces are enabling corporate security forces.

Fortunately, the water protectors were more politically savvy and more loving than those who were trying to provoke them.

On October 27, 2016, security forces unleashed a barrage of violent tactics against the water protectors, including pepper spray, tear gas bombs, grenades, and plastic bullets. Many were injured, but the water protectors responded by maintaining their prayerful and peaceful protest. Heavily militarized police from seven different states forcibly removed the protestors from their camp.

As video of all this was broadcast around the world, the response was mass outrage at the tactics of the security forces and their treatment of visibly nonviolent protestors. Montana County sheriff Brian Gootkin, who was on his way to Standing Rock with a detail of law enforcement officers to support the security forces there, received messages from all over the world as well as from his constituents in Montana objecting to the treatment of the water protectors. Sheriff Gootkin said, "I just don't understand where we separated from the public. It really breaks my heart. We are not the enemy." He and his forces turned around and went back to Montana. The outcry in Minnesota was so great that Sheriff Rich Stanek's deputies went home. Wisconsin Sheriff Dave Mahoney and his officers left Standing Rock after one week and refused to return. Law enforcement personnel from other states responded in similar ways.[13]

The Standing Rock water protectors demonstrated that it is still possible to resist nonviolently and win people's hearts, even when state forces think they understand nonviolent action well enough to defeat it. Love is still more powerful than hate.

Responding from the Heart

We can study the strategy and tactics of nonviolence and practice its principles, such as resisting *agents provocateurs*, but in the end it often comes down to a spontaneous response of the heart to other human beings and a willingness to lay down our lives for them:

During a period of terrible riots some years ago in Gujarat (Gandhi's home state) a "Hindu" mob descended on a rural village, primed to kill. Almost all the village men were out in the fields. The women reacted quickly, however, and took in their Muslim neighbors to hide them from the mob. As they lived mostly in one room cottages, it often meant "hiding" the Muslims in the *puja* corner, underneath their household altar. The mob stormed up to home after home screaming, "You're hiding Muslims in there!" "Yes," the woman calmly replied. "We are coming in to get them!" Then the women, one after the other said, "First kill me, then only you may enter." Every Muslim in the village was saved that day.[14]

Reflection Process

1. Close your eyes and put your feet flat on the floor. Breathe slowly and deeply. Place your hand on your heart and imagine that you are breathing in and out through your heart.

2. Get in touch with someone you once disliked or even hated, and who is now your friend. What happened to help you experience this person as a human being much like yourself, rather than an enemy?

3. As you continue to breathe in and out through your heart, breathe into yourself the willingness and capacity to find your common humanity with all people.

Reflection Questions

What touched me most in this chapter is . . .
When I reflect on this chapter in relation to my life, I feel . . .
I want . . .

Chapter 8

"But It Wouldn't Have Worked Against the Nazis": Denmark

The Nazis . . . had met resistance based on principle, and their "toughness" had melted like butter in the sun.

Hannah Arendt[1]

The most common objection to nonviolent action is, "But it wouldn't have worked against the Nazis." Therefore, of all the examples of successful active nonviolence during the twentieth century, we have chosen Denmark (in this chapter) and the village of Le Chambon-sur-Lignon, France (chapter 9), which were two of the largest nonviolent resistance operations against the Nazis in Europe during World War II. They were not the only ones; as we have mentioned, nonviolent resistance to the Nazis was used successfully in other places, including Bulgaria, Finland, Norway, and Italy. We chose to focus on Denmark and Le Chambon in part because, in both cases, young people about John's age played a critical role and because we have visited both places.

Denmark

The Danes proved that however dreadful the opponent faced by those using nonviolent action, If resistance is resilient and imaginative, military sanctions are not

enough to stamp out a popular movement—and violent reprisals may only harden the opposition. . . . If the
Nazis, the cruelest killing machine in the century's history, could be kept off balance by Danish schoolboys,
amateur saboteurs, and underground clergymen, what
other regime should be thought invulnerable to nonviolent resistance?[2]

The Nazis invaded Denmark, a country of about 3.8 million,
on April 9, 1940.[3] They took over the whole country in less than
six hours without firing a shot.[4] The Danish government was
told that if they submitted without resistance, Germany would
allow them to maintain their political independence and their
territorial integrity.[5] The Germans were willing to treat Denmark with more respect than other occupied countries because
they wanted Danish labor, natural resources, and agricultural
products,[6] and also because they wanted to be on good terms
with a people they regarded as "fellow Aryans."[7]

The Danish king Christian X and his ministers settled on
a policy of cooperation with Germany, because they thought
this would allow them to maintain as much as possible of their
national life and self-rule. However, their attitude was not one
of surrender.[8] Underneath the official policy, the Danes strongly
objected to cooperating with the Germans. Their pride in their
country was offended, and they felt unwilling to be humiliated.
They never had to follow Gandhi's first step of nonviolent resistance, moving from passivity and submission to courage and
self-respect, because they never gave up their courage and self-
respect to the Germans.

The Danes automatically challenged the source of power
that Sharp refers to as *authority*, since their internal stance
toward the Germans was not one of submission. They also
challenged the source of power that Sharp calls *attitudes* or
beliefs, because their patriotic beliefs were directed toward
Denmark, not Germany.

Seventeen-year-old Arne Sejr
Inspires the Resistance

When the Nazis invaded, seventeen-year-old Arne Sejr, an ordinary Danish schoolboy, was outraged, and he wrote "Ten Commandments for Danes:"

1. You must not go to work in Germany and Norway.
2. You shall do a bad job for the Germans.
3. You shall work slowly for the Germans.
4. You shall destroy important machines and tools.
5. You shall destroy everything which may be of benefit to the Germans.
6. You shall delay all transport.
7. You shall boycott German and Italian films and papers.
8. You must not shop at Nazis' stores.
9. You shall treat traitors for what they are worth.
10. You shall protect anyone chased by the Germans.

Join the struggle for the freedom of Denmark![9]

Arne typed twenty-five copies and sent them to influential people in his town and to high school students all over the country. His commandments were passed from one person to another and "eventually became sacred to the Danes, as they waged their national resistance."[10] During the course of the German occupation, the Danish people would carry out most or all of Arne's commandments.

They began with community song festivals in the parks, where hundreds of thousands of people sang national anthems.[11] An underground press developed to share truthful information with the Danes, and this helped unite them in a spirit of resistance. The press reached 2.6 million people, which was the entire adult population of Denmark.[12]

Throughout the occupation, King Christian was the Danes' emotional and spiritual leader. As he had done before the war, the king rode his horse every day, unescorted, through the streets of Copenhagen. The Danish people gathered along his route to applaud or shake his hand. German soldiers stood watching, but King Christian turned his gaze away from them. The bishop of Copenhagen said of the king, "He sustains us, he unites us, he guides us."[13] The mutual love and respect between King Christian and his people undermined any German claim to authority and, along with the underground press, helped inoculate the Danish people against Nazi propaganda.

As the Germans imposed more of their policies, such as recruiting Danish men into the military, Danish resistance grew. This included acts of sabotage. For example, Danish schoolboys put sugar in Nazi gas tanks and blew up a freight train loaded with war materials. Their slogan was, "If the adults won't do something, we will."[14] Factory workers worked really slowly. At the shipyards, they sabotaged the building of ships for the Germans, so they were never finished.[15] In this way, they undermined the Germans' source of power, which Sharp calls *material resources*.

Beginning in 1943, workers went on strike, and everything shut down.[16] In response to the strikes and sabotage, on August 28, 1943, the Germans demanded that strikes be banned, curfews imposed, and saboteurs executed. Parliament refused and went home, and the cabinet resigned.[17] The Germans imposed martial law, and Hitler ordered the imposition of racial laws in Denmark.[18] They wanted to segregate the Jews, but King Christian was adamant in his support of the Jewish community, and he refused to establish a ghetto for them. He said that if there were such a ghetto, he and his family would move from their palace to be with their Jews. The Nazis backed down, and there was no Jewish ghetto in Denmark.[19]

The Rescue of the Jews

There were nearly eight thousand Jews in Denmark at this time, or 0.2 percent of the population. Fifteen hundred of them were refugees from Germany and Eastern Europe.[20] In August, 1943, the Germans planned a surprise roundup of the Jews for the evening of Friday, October 1, 1943. It was the evening of Rosh Hashanah, the Jewish New Year, when all the Jews would be at home celebrating.

George Duckwitz, a Nazi official, found out about the plan and did not agree with it. Duckwitz is a striking example of undermining the source of power that Gene Sharp calls *human resources*, meaning those who propped up the rulers. Although Duckwitz had been part of the Nazi leadership, he ultimately refused to support the Nazi's plans for the Jews. Instead, Duckwitz revealed the Nazi plan to Danish leaders, who warned the Jewish community.

Jewish leaders organized a messenger service to tell all the Jews to go into hiding.[21] The country united in opposition to the roundup of their Jews, about 1,500 of whom (the refugees from other countries) were not even Danish citizens:

> The news spread like lightning, thanks in part to many non-Jewish Danes. Ambulance driver Jorgen Knudsen searched through local phone books for the addresses of families with "Jewish-sounding names." He then drove his ambulance to go warn them and, if they had nowhere to hide, took them either to the hospital or to homes of doctors active in the resistance. Other Jews were approached on the street by total strangers who offered them keys to their apartments or houses. . . . Denmark's Jews had slipped away "behind a living wall raised by the Danish people in the space of one night."[22]

Jews were hidden in attics and basements, but the only really safe place for them was Sweden, which was neutral during the war. Rescue groups sprang up to transport the Jews to the coast, where they were carried in fishing boats across the Baltic Sea to Sweden. The rescuers used the code word "potatoes" to refer to Jewish refugees; for example, "Eighteen sacks of potatoes are ready to be picked up."[23] The solidarity of the Danish people on behalf of the Jews was so great that when money was needed for rescue operations, "you simply went to a bank and asked the teller for 5,000 or 10,000 kroner, stating your purpose, and the money was promptly handed to you." There is no record that anyone ever took advantage of this for their own personal gain.[24]

The rescue almost did not succeed. Word came that the king of Sweden was afraid that giving asylum to the Jews would compromise Swedish neutrality. However, the famous Danish physicist, Niels Bohr, who was hiding out in Uppsala, Sweden, found out about the king's threatened refusal to give asylum. He sent word to the Swedish king that if the Jews were not taken in, he would surrender himself to the Nazis. The king relented and accepted the Jews.[25]

In this way, about 7,200 Jews escaped to Sweden, where they stayed until the war ended and they could safely return to Denmark. Most found their homes and businesses as they had left them, because of the care of the Danish people.[26]

Isaac and Mona

As we were completing this book, we visited Denmark to learn more about the rescue of the Jews. We were introduced to Isaac and Mona, a couple who were saved as children along with their families. They told us how they were taken in small fishing boats to Sweden. Mona remembered seeing soldiers in green uniforms as they neared the Swedish coast, and feared they were Nazis. But, she said, as soon as she heard them say, "Welcome to Sweden," she knew they were Swedish soldiers and that she and her family would be safe. She remembers how well cared for she and her family were in Sweden . . . even bananas to eat! And she remembers that on the day before they left Denmark, it was her birthday and the neighbors who helped rescue her family made a cake to celebrate.

We were most impressed by how vibrant and healthy Isaac and Mona appeared. Isaac is ninety years old, Mona is in her eighties, and they both look much younger. We think they represent the ability to endure hardship in an environment of care, as the Danes provided them. Also, neither Isaac nor Mona was separated from their families, and these unbroken bonds of love seem to have shielded them from the emotional trauma carried by many holocaust survivors.

The Danes Advocate for Their Jews

The Germans captured only about 470 Jews in Denmark and deported them to Theresienstadt ghetto in Czechoslovakia. The Danish authorities and the Danish Red Cross insistently demanded information about what was happening to these Jews, and this probably deterred the Germans from sending them to extermination camps. In the end, only about seventy of the Jews died, mostly from sickness, or less than 1 percent of the Jewish population in Denmark.[27]

This was the lowest of any of the German-occupied countries in Europe. In Poland, the Netherlands, and France, for example, armed resistance to the Nazis was unsuccessful, and the death of Jews in those countries was much higher. In France, 26 percent of 300,000 Jews were killed; in the Netherlands, 75 percent of 140,000 Jews were killed; and in Poland, 90 percent of 3.3 million Jews were killed.[28]

Poland: Collaboration Rather Than Advocacy

Among those Polish Jews who died were many of my (Sheila's) ancestors. My father escaped from Poland to the United States, along with his three older sisters and their parents. His younger sister, Anne, was born in the United States. All these aunts of mine lived in Los Angeles, and I went to visit them while I was studying theology in Berkeley. I stayed with Anne, who was very worried about my visiting her older sisters. Assuming I was a Christian, she said, "Please, at least don't wear a cross when you go to see them, because it will frighten them." And then she told me why.

Anne said that when her sisters were children in Poland, Easter Sunday was a holiday for the Polish soldiers. For their recreation, the soldiers would go out and hunt Jews with bayonets. My aunts' memories of Easter Sunday were of hiding from the soldiers in terror in the basement. That is what the cross meant to them.

Why did the Poles collaborate with the Germans in this way, and why did the Danes refuse to collaborate, even risking their lives to save their Jews? Perhaps chapters 12 and 13 of this book can at least give us some clues.

Mass Resistance

The Danes were encouraged in their nonviolent resistance by their successful rescue of the Jews. The resistance grew stronger, and underground militias were formed that avoided human targets but did use weapons to attack railroad lines and German military equipment and supplies. Many teachers of active nonviolence believe that the destruction of property is a form of violence and therefore counterproductive. The Danish resistance leader Frode Jakobsen seems to have agreed. He understood what Chenoweth and Stephan would later emphasize, that the destruction of property during a nonviolent campaign diminishes the chances of success (see page 25), and that mass participation is more likely to the extent that a movement is entirely nonviolent:

> [He] ... believed the resistance should be accessible to all citizens, most of whom had to live above ground. He wanted an entire society opposing the Germans, not merely a group of armed gunman, just as Gandhi had understood that if a foreign occupier were to be opposed effectively, people from all walks of life had to enlist.

When a greater part of the population turned against the foreign force—when they withdrew their consent—then it would have neither the cooperation it needed to govern nor the legitimacy to pretend to do so.[29]

Resistance leaders realized that nonviolent resistance was more effective: "Violence by the resistance had not seriously weakened the Germans, but violence against the people had roused the nation to take massive nonviolent action—and the resistance leaders hastened to catch up."[30] Their favorite and most effective nonviolent method was strikes. Large portions of the population would be willing to participate in strikes, whereas most people did not want to participate in any form of violence, including blowing things up.

Even though strikes had been banned, workers continued them on a massive scale by saying they had to go home early to water their gardens and could not do it after work because of the curfew. The "Go Home Early" movement spread and led to a general strike.[31] This crippled the manufacture of vehicles for the German army.[32] Once again, the Danes had undermined the material resources of the Germans as a source of their power.

The Germans backed down and ended the curfew. The Danes had learned what Gandhi believed, what Gene Sharp later emphasized, and what the research of Erica Chenoweth and Maria Stephan has confirmed, about the value of noncooperation on a mass scale: a people's greatest weapon is the withdrawal of obedience.[33] Nationwide strikes continued.

In 1944, the Germans decided that the Danish police could not be trusted, and they arrested ten thousand of them. They went to the castle, arrested the king's police entourage, and threatened to raise the swastika.

When a German officer informed the king that he had orders to raise the swastika over the castle, the king refused and exclaimed, "If this happens, a Danish soldier will go and take it down." "That Danish soldier will be shot," the

officer replied. "That Danish soldier will be myself," the
king responded. The swastika never flew over the castle.[34]

In May 1945, Germany surrendered. Denmark emerged from
the war in relatively good condition, both socially and economi-
cally, because the Danes had found a way to resist without
introducing violence into their society, which might have torn
them apart and diminished them as a people. To the contrary,
they offered the Germans an example of genuine strength.

The Danes remembered who they were, and their goodness
was greater than the power of violence. "Denmark had not won
the war, but neither had it been defeated or destroyed. Most
Danes had not been brutalized, by the Germans or by each
other. Nonviolence saved the country and contributed to the
Allied victory, more than Danish arms ever could have."[35]

Reflection Process

1. Close your eyes and put your feet flat on the floor. Breathe
slowly and deeply. Place your hand on your heart and imagine
that you are breathing in and out through your heart.

2. If you had lived in Denmark during the German occupation, what role do you imagine you would have taken? Would
you have been a Dane, and if so what would you have done?
How might you have resisted the Nazis? Would you have
helped the Jews, and if so, how? Would you have been a Jew
who escaped? What do you imagine that was like?

3. As you continue to breathe in and out through your heart,
breathe into yourself whatever you might have needed to survive in this situation without being brutalized.

Reflection Questions

What touched me most in this chapter is . . .
When I reflect on this chapter in relation to my life, I feel . . .
I want . . .

Chapter 9

"But It Wouldn't Have Worked Against the Nazis": Le Chambon-sur-Lignon

A woman whose three children were saved in the village of Le Chambon said, "The Holocaust was storm, lightning, thunder, wind, rain, yes. And Le Chambon was the rainbow." The rainbow is . . . a promise that living will have the last word, not killing. The rainbow means realistic hope. For that woman, whose three daughters were saved by the villagers of Le Chambon, history is not hopeless because of the unshakeable fact that lives were saved in Le Chambon.

Philip Hallie[1]

Denmark is an entire country that did not collaborate with the Nazis. Le Chambon-sur-Lignon is a small village in a country that did collaborate. Le Chambon is located in southern France, which was the so-called Free Zone during World War II. It was administered by the Vichy government, led by Marshal Pétain. Pétain enforced increasing restrictions on Jews. At first they were sent to internment camps, and later they were deported to Nazi extermination camps.[2]

During the war, Le Chambon was a small village of approximately five thousand people. They were mostly poor, uneducated farmers, descendants of the Huguenots, who had been persecuted for their religion. During the four years of the

German occupation of France, "Le Chambon became the safest place for Jews in Europe."[3] The people of Le Chambon saved the lives of about five thousand Jewish refugees, most of them children.

André Trocmé

Like the Danes, the Chambonnais had an inspired and beloved leader, André Trocmé. Trocmé was born in 1901 and, like the people of Le Chambon, was descended from the Huguenots. When he was a young boy, his father accidentally killed his mother in a car accident. Trocmé

> learned the preciousness of the victim's life and the preciousness of the slayer's life. For the rest of his life . . . he would eschew the vicious circle of revenge. The loss death inflicted was too awesome to be perpetrated upon any human being. Life was too precious—all human life.[4]

Trocmé believed that "the plague of mankind is . . . man's willingness to allow killing to happen without resisting it."[5]

Trocmé married Magda Grilli, an Italian woman who shared his desire to help humanity. After he completed seminary training in the United States, he served as a pastor elsewhere in France, and then he and his family moved to Le Chambon, where he was their pastor throughout the war. During the Nazi occupation, Trocmé was the leader of nonviolent resistance in his region of France.[6] He preached love for everyone and the obligation to avoid doing anything to cause harm and to prevent others from causing harm.

The Chambonnais: Amateurs at Saving Lives

The Chambonnais were simple, good, generous people, who understood what it was like to be persecuted, and they would not turn away from anyone who was in danger. As Le Chambon became known as a safe place for Jews, more and more of them came there, and underground relief agencies placed children there. The Chambonnais took in anyone who needed shelter, often for several years, and shared the little food they had: "no Chambonnais ever turned away a refugee; no Chambonnais ever denounced or betrayed a refugee."[7]

André and Magda Trocmé had a team of people who worked together to watch over the sheltering of Jewish refugees and to alert them when there was danger from nearby Nazis. Nevertheless, much of what happened was a spontaneous response of the people to the plight of the Jews. The people of Le Chambon were untrained in nonviolent resistance, and they were "amateurs at saving lives." All they had was "love for their fellow human beings" and "an alert common sense."[8] Trocmé was their leader, but his preaching matched their own human instincts.

The people of Le Chambon believed that they could and must say no to indignity and tyranny, and Trocmé taught them that if they said no, then creative ways of carrying out their resistance would open up to them. For example, when word came that government officials had insisted the villagers gather every morning and salute the flag using the Nazi salute, the people refused to salute the correct way. Eventually, they stopped gathering at all to salute the flag.[9] They would not let the Nazis steal their consciences:

> Following their consciences meant refusing to hate or kill any human being . . . human life was too precious to them to be taken for any reason. . . . Their consciences told them to save as many lives as they could, even if doing this meant endangering the lives of all the villagers; and they obeyed their consciences.[10]

Thus, the Chambonnais undermined the source of power that Sharp identifies as *sanctions*, meaning enforcing obedience through the threat of punishment, because they were willing to risk imprisonment or death in order to follow their consciences. As it turned out, the Nazis were either unaware of or ignored the refusal of the villagers to use the Nazi salute, which further emboldened the Chambonnais.[11]

Teenagers Forge Documents

The creativity of the Chambonnais's resistance included the forging of documents, such as passports. These were needed to allow Jewish refugees to travel to safer places than France, such as Switzerland. A seventeen-year-old Jewish boy, Oscar Rosowsky, and his friend, another young boy, appeared in Le Chambon. Oscar was a gifted forger. He made about fifty documents a day and gave them to the family who sheltered him. They hid the documents in their beehives. When they became afraid that the Germans might search the beehives, the family hid the forged documents in a family grave in back of their house. Oscar was never caught, and eventually became a physician.[12]

Satyagraha = Love in Action

Although the Chambonnais had not studied Gandhi's concept of *satyagraha*, they understood instinctively the principles of love in action and overcoming evil with good (perhaps for reasons we will discuss in chapters 12 and 13). Trocmé and his team reinforced this based on Christian values.[13] The people had probably never studied the teachings of Gandhi, but they believed they should prevent harm to anyone, both the Jews and the Nazis. "They were trying to protect the victims, but they were also trying to stop human beings who were hell-bent on becoming victimizers, hell-bent on doing evil."[14]

The Chambonnais understood the two hands, and used them. With one hand they said to the Nazi collaborators, "No, you cannot harm our Jews." With the other they said, "Yes, you, too, are human, and we care about you. It is not good for you to hurt other human beings."

Kinship vs. Difference

One of the characteristics of the Chambonnais, which seems to have contributed to their willingness to risk their lives for strangers in need, was the closeness of their community. They were totally united and supportive of one another. Another characteristic was their unwillingness to see other human beings as different from themselves.

In contrast, the basis of Nazism was emphasizing difference by dividing people into "one of us" and "one of them."[15] They explicitly tried to eliminate the sense of kinship that leads to justice (see chapter 1). The official handbook of the Hitler Youth Organization said, "The foundation of the National Socialist outlook on life is the perception of the unlikeness of men."[16] The Germans taught that those of Aryan blood were precious and Jews were not.

The French who collaborated with the Nazis also divided people, but the people of Le Chambon did not. Their attitude was, "We do not know what a Jew is. We know only men."[17] The Nazis could not understand this, and when they interrogated André Trocmé's cousin, Daniel, as to whether he was helping Jews, they said to him, "You must be one of them—otherwise you could not defend them so."[18]

The Chambonnais, who saw only human beings, treated the Jews as their own, while also respecting their Jewish faith. For example, the Chambonnais never tried to convert the Jews to Christianity, and a Jewish survivor who was sheltered in Le Chambon recalled that the Chambonnais helped the Jews celebrate their Jewish holidays.[19]

Invisible Protection

The Nazis knew that Jews were hidden in Le Chambon, and they referred to it as "that nest of Jews in Huguenot country."[20] The Germans and their French collaborators were rounding up Jews all over France throughout the occupation, but, with one exception, they did not round up the Jews of Le Chambon. The exception was a raid by the Gestapo in Le Chambon on Daniel Trocmé's house, in which a small group of Jewish refugees was captured.[21] Daniel was captured, as well, and he died on April 4, 1944, at the Maidanek concentration camp in Poland (along with many of Sheila's ancestors).[22]

Otherwise, there seemed to be some sort of invisible protection around the village. Major Schmehling, a German officer who was urged to attack Le Chambon and did not do so, was interviewed after the war. He said, "This kind of resistance had nothing to do with violence, nothing to do with anything we could destroy with violence."[23]

A Conspiracy of Goodness

By saving their Jews, Le Chambon, like Denmark, accomplished what seemed impossible in the face of Nazi brutality. The two peoples shared inspired beloved leaders (André Trocmé and King Christian X), compassion, stubbornness in the face of oppression, too much self-respect to allow themselves to be humiliated, and a close, healthy society. The Chambonnais were united more by their religious faith and the Danes more by national pride. Both were united in their solidarity on behalf of the Jews, whom they saw as kin—human beings just like themselves.

When the people of Le Chambon were interviewed later and praised for what they had done, they said,

> How can you call us good? We were doing what had to be done. Who else could help them? . . . Things had to be done, that's all, and we happened to be there to do them. You must understand that it was the most natural thing in the world to help these people.[24]

Magda Trocmé called it "a conspiracy of goodness."[25]

Reflection Process

1. Close your eyes and put your feet flat on the floor. Breathe slowly and deeply. Place your hand on your heart and imagine that you are breathing in and out through your heart.

2. If you were a Nazi stationed in France in the region of Le Chambon, and you received an order to round up the Jews who were hidden there, what would you have done?

3. As you continue to breathe in and out through your heart, breathe into yourself whatever you might have needed to survive in this situation and be able to live with yourself.

Reflection Questions

What touched me most in this chapter is . . .

When I reflect on this chapter in relation to my life, I feel . . . I want . . .

Chapter 10

SOA Watch

There is nothing wrong with a traffic law which says you have to stop for a red light. But when a fire is raging, the fire truck goes right through that red light, and normal traffic had better get out of the way. Or, when a man is bleeding to death, the ambulance goes through those red lights at top speed. There is a fire raging now. . . . Disinherited people all over the world are bleeding to death from deep social and economic wounds. They need brigades of ambulance drivers who will have to ignore the red lights of the present system until the emergency is solved.

Martin Luther King Jr.[1]

As another example of active nonviolence, we have chosen the annual demonstration to close the U.S. military's School of the Americas (SOA), now the Western Hemisphere Institute for Security Cooperation (WHINSEC), at Fort Benning, Georgia. We chose this because we have seen first-hand in Guatemala the impact of the SOA in Latin America, because we all participated in the demonstration in 2008, and because it was such a formative experience for John, who was eleven at the time.

The School of the Americas was founded as a training school for Latin American soldiers. It was established in Panama in 1946 and moved to Fort Benning, Georgia, in 1984. In 2001, it was renamed Western Hemisphere Institute for Security Cooperation.[2] Since its founding, the school has trained over 64,000 Latin American soldiers in counterinsurgency techniques, including methods of torture, which are encouraged in SOA/ WHINSEC training manuals.[3]

Graduates of the school have been involved in some of the worst human rights abuses in Latin America. These include the 1980 rape and murder of four American nuns who were working with the poor; the murder of Archbishop Oscar Romero, also in 1980; and the murder of six Jesuit priests, their housekeeper, and her daughter in 1989. All these crimes took place in El Salvador, but graduates of SOA/WHINSEC have also been responsible for torture, assassinations, and massacres throughout Latin America. This includes the thousands of *desaparecidos* in Argentina mentioned in the Prologue and genocide in Guatemala.[4]

Genocide in Guatemala

In the Prologue, we described the work of our friend, Andrea. The Guatemalan soldiers who terrorized the people of her mountain village, as well as other Mayan villages throughout the country, were led by graduates of the School of the Americas. Under their rule, between 1960 and 1996 an estimated 250,000 native Mayan people were killed, many of them women and children. The worst of this was in the 1980s, during the dictatorship of General Efrain Rios Montt, who overthrew the government in 1982.[5]

Rios Montt and much of his cabinet were SOA graduates, as were other military leaders who helped Rios Montt develop a scorched-earth policy that wiped out entire villages.[6] In 1999, a U.N.-sponsored commission concluded that the U.S.-backed Guatemalan army had committed genocide.[7] Children were often the primary targets in village massacres, and more than 200,000 children lost one or both parents.[8]

We saw the results of this in a village near the coast, where Andrea sent us to learn more about the genocide perpetrated by SOA graduates. In that village, there were no fathers—only widowed mothers. All the men, who had tried to organize for better working conditions, which threatened the economic power of U.S. corporations, had been killed by the Guatemalan army. The women were left with no way to support themselves or their children. Andrea's missionary friends who worked in that village encouraged the widows to form a weavings co-op. They found sympathetic people in the United States who would sell the weavings at fair prices and send all the income back to the widows. We volunteered to help, and for several years we sold the weavings at our retreats.

As soon as I (John) was old enough, I supervised the sale of weavings. When I was fourteen, we visited that same village again, and I met some of the women who made the beautiful weavings. While we were there, a team of American eye doctors came to treat the villagers, and I volunteered to help with Spanish translation. Besides having eye conditions, everyone we treated appeared weak and sick, and I saw firsthand the poverty and vulnerability of these people. They still live with the devastation of their culture, caused in large part by graduates of the SOA.

The Founding of SOA Watch

Like us, our friend Roy Bourgeois had seen the effects of SOA graduates on Latin America. We (Denny and Sheila) knew and trusted Roy from when we attended language school with him in Bolivia before John was born, and we followed his work.

After the six Jesuits were murdered in El Salvador, Roy and a small group of others founded SOA Watch, an organization whose purpose is to educate the public about what graduates of the school are doing in Latin America and lobby members of Congress to close the school. Members of SOA Watch understand that SOA/WHINSEC graduates are being used to control the people and the resources of Latin America on behalf of the U.S. government and the large corporations whose interests our

government often serves. These corporations seek to appropri-
ate land and extract resources in Latin America for their own
benefit, without regard for the well-being of the native people.

Members of the small upper-class in these countries, who
often have ties to U.S. corporations, are allowed to remain
rich. The poor, however, who try to protect their land and its
resources, are targeted by their country's military, many of
whom were trained at the SOA/WHINSEC to enforce U.S. economic policy. When the U.S. signs trade agreements with Latin
American countries, these agreements normally benefit the corporations but hurt the poor, who try to protest in some way.
Then even more soldiers from those countries are sent to SOA/
WHINSEC to be trained to enforce the trade agreements.[9]

In 1995, SOA Watch instituted an annual vigil at the main
entrance to Fort Benning on or around November 16, the anni-
versary of the massacre of the Jesuits.[10] Those who choose to
cross the line onto Fort Benning property are arrested. Thus far,
about three hundred protesters have spent a combined total of
over 150 years in federal prisons or local jails for their actions at
the demonstration.[11]

My Experience at the SOA Watch Vigil

I (John) attended the SOA Watch Vigil in 2008 with my parents. There were about twenty thousand other demonstrators
that year. I remember how well organized the demonstration
was, even with so many people who had come from all over
the world. As far as I saw, everyone was kind and friendly to
one another. The atmosphere was a combination of solemnity
and fun. For instance, there was street theater, with people in
costumes on stilts, and music.

Each participant was given a simple, white, wooden cross
with the name and age on it of someone from Latin America
who had been murdered at the hands of SOA/WHINSEC
graduates. I still have mine; it says, "Ruperto Chicas, 40 años."

The main activity was a procession down a roadway toward the gates of Fort Benning, where many participants hung their white crosses on the wire fence. Also on the fence was the jacket from an American soldier's uniform, with a note pinned on it that said:

> To Whom It May Concern:
> I wore this jacket with honor for 20 years, but I am returning it for I have learned that it does not represent duty, honor, or country. The military's main objective is to expand and protect capitalism. In other words, it is used to protect the elite.
> Sincerely,
> Donna D. Stevens
> I am a patriot too!

I volunteered for a special part of the procession that simulated a funeral. About twenty of us, all adults except me, put on black robes and our faces were painted white. We carried cardboard caskets up to the gates, as people chanted. We then lay down on a grassy area in front of the gates, and some of the organizers sprayed us with red paint that looked like blood. We stayed there for about half an hour, to dramatize the death and destruction caused by SOA/WHINSEC graduates.

The effect on my life of participating in the SOA Watch Vigil has been a deeper understanding of the brutality of violence and its consequences for the lives of human beings. I attended a session for kids given by an American Jesuit who was visiting El Salvador when the six Jesuits, their housekeeper, and her daughter were murdered. He saw the scene of the massacre shortly after it happened, including the dead bodies, and he described it to us. I was shocked. My parents and I did not have television at home, so I had not grown up seeing extreme violence. I could not comprehend how any human being could do such things to others. I resolved that I would never participate in such violence myself.

I was also deeply moved by the courage of the people I met at the demonstration who care so much that they have gone to places like El Salvador themselves. One of them was a college friend of my mother. His daughter is about my age, and I met her at the session for kids. My mother's college friend knew the six Jesuits, and he could have been killed along with them. I hope I will have that kind of courage if I am ever in a situation that calls for it.

The School of the Americas and Immigration

In 2016, SOA Watch held a demonstration at the Arizona border, in addition to the one at Ft. Benning. They went to the Arizona border because border control agents are now being sent to WHINSEC. One of the reasons for training border agents in methods of torture and interrogation at WHINSEC involves the relationship between immigration and efforts of the U.S. government to control the resources of Latin America.

For example, in 2009 the United States enabled a military coup in Honduras, led by SOA graduates, to overturn the government of democratically elected President Manuel Zelaya. Zelaya's policies, such as raising the minimum wage, would have undermined the profits of large corporations in Honduras and elsewhere in the region. Such corporations see countries like Honduras as opportunities for business ventures in mining, logging, agribusiness, hydropower, and tourism. Poor Honduran people who try to protect their land and its resources from those corporations are now being imprisoned or assassinated by SOA/WHINSEC graduates.[12]

This has created a climate of violence and terror in Honduras, and many Hondurans desperately seek to save their lives and the lives of their children by trying to cross the border into the United States.[13] The journey is a dangerous one, and some people attempt it by riding on the tops of trains. The last time we were in Mexico, we worked with hospital volunteers who care for Honduran refugees who had fallen off those trains.

More border control agents are now being trained at WHIN-SEC to "deal with" Hondurans trying to enter the United States. This is why SOA Watch wanted to hold a demonstration at the border. As Hendrick Voss, national organizer for SOA Watch, told us,

> If the border patrol goes to WHINSEC, we'll go to the border. We want to address the consequences of the coup in Honduras and its effect on immigration. We want to provide education relevant to what's happening *now*, and now it's the relationship between WHINSEC and immigration. For us to be effective, we have to address the critical issue of the root cause of migration, which is U.S. sponsored militarization and violence throughout Latin America.[14]

Accomplishments

As a result of SOA Watch, five countries—Argentina, Venezuela, Bolivia, Nicaragua, and Ecuador—have stopped sending soldiers to WHINSEC. Additionally, some members of Congress have become sympathetic to the cause of SOA Watch, and they have tried to cut off funding for WHINSEC. Thus far, they have succeeded in reducing military aid to Honduras.[15] SOA Watch's long-term goal is to close WHINSEC.

When I (John) asked Hendrik what the SOA Watch Vigil has accomplished, he spoke about the many thousands of people who have been educated about U.S. foreign policy in Latin America. They have also learned about active nonviolence, and many of them have committed themselves to social justice as a life goal. They include me and my parents.

Reflection Process

1. Close your eyes and put your feet flat on the floor. Breathe slowly and deeply. Place your hand on your heart and imagine that you are breathing in and out through your heart.

2. Imagine that you are an undocumented immigrant to the United States from Latin America. What is the story of why you came and how you got here? What do you most need to feel at home, and what do you have to give?

3. Imagine that you are a border control agent. What is the story of why you became one? What do you most need to feel at home within yourself, and what do you have to give?

4. As you continue to breathe in and out through your heart, breathe in the love and care you need in situations where you do not feel safe or at home.

Reflection Questions

What touched me most in this chapter is . . .

When I reflect on this chapter in relation to my life, I feel . . . I want . . .

Chapter 11

What Works

If the method of violence takes plenty of training, the method of nonviolence takes even more training, and that training is much more difficult than the training for violence.

Mohandas Gandhi[1]

In the preceding three chapters we presented three examples of active nonviolence. Two were highly successful, Denmark and Le Chambon. The third, SOA Watch, has been only partially successful, since WHINSEC has not yet been closed. What factors contributed to these outcomes?

Undermining the Six Sources of Power

Although neither Denmark nor Le Chambon had ever heard of Gene Sharp, they seem to have instinctively understood the strategy and tactics that he would later articulate. Besides maintaining their dignity and self-respect, they cleverly undermined the Nazis' sources of power: authority, human resources, skills and knowledge, attitudes or beliefs, material resources, and sanctions.

For example, the Danes challenged any claim to authority the Nazis might have had by providing accurate information through the underground press that reached the entire adult population of the country. They coopted a key human resource of the Nazis, in the person of the German official George

Duckwitz, when he became willing to disclose his knowledge of the Nazis' plans to round up the Danish Jews. This enabled the Danes to save the Jews. The Danes' attitude of obedience was not to the Nazis, but rather to their own resistance leaders, who cultivated this by treating people with respect. They used strikes and working slowly at the shipyards to undermine the Germans' material resources. Finally, the Danes were not intimidated by Nazi threats of sanctions such as imprisonment or execution.

Like the Danes, the Chambonnais did not recognize the authority of the Nazis. Perhaps because of their long history of persecution by religious authorities, the people of Le Chambon had learned to think for themselves and trust their own inner moral sense. Their attitudes and beliefs emphasized care for other human beings rather than obedience or patriotism. Their goodness seems to have infected the human resources of the Nazis, such as the Nazi troops who were stationed in or near Le Chambon and evidently ignored the evidence before their eyes that Jews were being sheltered there. Finally, sanctions meant nothing to the Chambonnais; they were quite willing to die in order to protect the Jews.

Sooner Rather Than Later

According to teacher of active nonviolence Michael Nagler, the longer violence has been allowed to go on unchecked, the more "soul force" and sacrifice it will take to stop it.[2] In both Denmark and Le Chambon, resistance to the Nazis was immediate. While the Danes feigned cooperation at first, the people were quickly united in their resistance. Although some Danes engaged in the destruction of property, such as railroad tracks, the cycle of violence was never well established, and resistance leaders quickly realized that nonviolent action was more effective because everyone could participate. In Le Chambon, violence against anyone was totally contrary to the beliefs of the people, and it was never used.

Mass Participation

In their study of 323 campaigns, Chenoweth and Stephan emphasized mass participation as the single greatest factor in the success of nonviolent campaigns compared to violent ones.[3] They give 3.5 percent of the population as a critical mass for success. Remarkably, in Denmark and Le Chambon, virtually the entire population participated in nonviolent resistance to the Nazis.

SOA Watch

Like Denmark and Le Chambon, the SOA Watch community also has trusted leaders, such as Roy Bourgeois and Hendrik Voss, who model and encourage persistence in protecting one's own dignity and unwillingness to be a victim. SOA Watch members are united by shared values of social justice. Because it came at a later time in the history of nonviolent resistance, SOA Watch has the advantage of learning from the experience of leaders such as Martin Luther King Jr. and theoreticians such as Gene Sharp.

The SOA Watch community understands the importance of undermining the opponent's sources of power, and a primary way they accomplish this is by disseminating accurate information that challenges the authority of the U.S. government by telling the truth about the role of the SOA/WHINSEC in Latin America. Another way is by refusing to be intimidated by sanctions such as imprisonment.

As in Denmark and Le Chambon, the cycle of violence was never established in SOA Watch—it never got going at all. Members of the SOA community are trained in not allowing themselves to be provoked into violence. They also understand and appreciate Gene Sharp's emphasis on careful planning, preparation, and training. They have been able to do this more than was possible in Denmark or Le Chambon. In those places, people found themselves in an emergency situation, and much of what happened was spontaneous, although the

leaders tried to catch up and provide what planning and preparation they could.

If we try to guess why SOA Watch has been only partially
successful in comparison with Denmark and Le Chambon, two
things stand out. The first is Chenoweth and Stephan's emphasis on mass participation. While participation in Le Chambon
and Denmark was far beyond 3.5 percent and, in fact, virtually
universal, only a very small percentage of the U.S. population
is even aware of SOA Watch, let alone participating. One reason
may be that most Americans, so far as they are aware, are not
affected personally. In comparison, during the Vietnam War,
every man of draft age, as well as his family and friends, had a
personal stake in that war, and a large portion of the population
was motivated to help end it.

Unlike those who resisted the Vietnam War, the twenty
thousand people whom we joined for the 2008 SOA Watch
demonstration, and even the many thousands of others who
supported us at home, are no match for the U.S. government
and its military forces. With only a tiny fraction of the population involved, it seems remarkable that SOA Watch has accomplished as much as it has in terms of influencing five Latin
American countries to stop sending their soldiers to WHINSEC
and influencing enough members of Congress to reduce military aid to Honduras.

A second factor that may have limited SOA Watch's effectiveness in comparison with Denmark and Le Chambon is that,
in both those places, the people lived side by side with the Jews
and saw their suffering and their vulnerability. The Jews were
friends and neighbors; neither the Danes nor the Chambonnais
were willing for them to be harmed. The Jews were constantly
"in the faces" of the Danes and the Chambonnais. In contrast,
Americans do not on a daily basis see the faces or the suffering
of Latin Americans whose lives are impacted by SOA graduates. We Americans have many ways to distract ourselves that
were not available to the Danes or the Chambonnais.

Despite the differences between the examples of nonviolent resistance that we have presented, what they have in common is the willingness of people to risk their freedom, their lives, or both on behalf of others.

Reflection Process

1. Close your eyes and put your feet flat on the floor. Breathe slowly and deeply. Place your hand on your heart and imagine that you are breathing in and out through your heart.
2. Of the three situations of active nonviolence that we have presented in the previous three chapters—Denmark, Le Chambon, and SOA Watch—which one moves or attracts you most deeply? Why?
3. As you continue to breathe in and out through your heart, breathe into yourself whatever growth or healing you may be experiencing as you learn about these examples of active nonviolence.

Reflection Questions

What touched me most in this chapter is . . .
When I reflect on this chapter in relation to my life, I feel . . .
I want . . .

Chapter 12

Why Do Some People Risk Their Lives for Others?

Nonviolence can be defined as remembering who we are . . . and constantly reclaiming the truth of reality—that we are all one . . . sisters and brothers of one another.

John Dear[1]

What makes it possible for human beings—such as the Standing Rock Sioux, the Danes, the Chambonnais, and the SOA Watch Vigil participants—to nonviolently risk their lives, their freedom, or both on behalf of others? Violence is "forgetting who we are."[2] When we remember who we are, we become capable of active nonviolence.

Remembering Who We Are

In Anthony Doerr's novel *All the Light We Cannot See,* one of the main characters is Werner, a German boy. He and his younger sister Jutta are raised in an orphanage by Frau Elena, a kindly Protestant nun who loves children and is kind to them. "Werner," she would say, "I believe in you. I think you'll do something great."[3] Werner passes on the kindness and empathy he receives from Frau Elena. For example, he brings fresh milk for the babies in the orphanage, and he cares for Jutta.

Because of his giftedness with radios, Werner is accepted into a school for Hitler Youth. The training is designed to make

Werner forget who he is. He is taught to despise weakness, as well as anyone who is different. According to the Nazis, only those who are racially pure are truly human. Jutta tries to tell him how hollow and empty the teachings of the Nazis are, but Werner does not listen to her.

The Nazis send Werner to Saint Malo, France, because the French resistance is active there through the use of radio transmissions. He is assigned to locate the radio operator so that his unit can kill that person. In a street in Saint Malo, Werner sees Marie-Laure, a blind French girl about his own age, and his heart opens to her. He figures out that her uncle is sending the radio transmissions from Saint Malo for the French resistance, but Werner's empathy for Marie-Laure moves him to protect her uncle and save her life at the risk of his own. "Jutta, he thinks, I finally listened."[4]

In caring for Marie-Laure, Werner remembers himself. In remembering himself, Werner recovers the qualities that the Nazis had tried to train out of him: empathy, altruism, and extensivity (a sense of kinship with a wide range of people). Research in the fields of neurology and psychology indicate that these qualities are innate to humans, although such qualities need a supportive environment in order to develop fully.[5]

Empathy, altruism, and extensivity are based on a sense of kinship with other human beings, rather than the sense of differentness that the Nazis taught. Kinship means seeing ourselves as part of a "we" rather than as an isolated "I."

Being a We: The Rescuers

When I (John) interviewed Hendrik Voss from SOA Watch, I noticed that whenever I asked him a question about himself, he kept moving from "I" to "we," and he spoke about the SOA Watch community. I realized that the basis of successful nonviolent action is being part of something bigger than yourself. They can stop an individual, but if you are part of a group, you have power.

The sense of being part of a "we" rather than an isolated "I" that I observed in Hendrik is consistent with the results of research on those who engage in active nonviolence on behalf of others.

The most extensive research on this has been done on the rescuers of Jews in Europe during World War II, primarily by Samuel and Pearl Oliner. Samuel was twelve years old when he escaped from a Polish ghetto—the only Jew who survived it—and was hidden from the Nazis by a peasant woman. Eventually, he came to America, became a professor of sociology, and married Pearl, a professor of education.[6]

Because so much of their activity was in secret, it is difficult to know the exact number, but there were an estimated 50,000 to 500,000 rescuers like the peasant woman who saved Samuel Oliner by hiding him in her home.[7] Studies of the rescuers indicate that they were characterized by high levels of empathy, altruism, and extensivity. All these qualities are based on the sense of "we" that John heard in Hendrik Voss. As one rescuer put it, "My father said the whole world is one big chain. One little part breaks and the chain is broken and it won't work anymore."[8]

Empathy, Altruism, and Extensivity

Empathy may be defined as

> the mental process by which one person enters into another's being and comes to know how they feel and think. . . . We enter into the emotional state of another's suffering and feel his or her pain as if it were our own . . . empathy conjures up active engagement . . .[9]

Rescuers were high in empathy for others' pain, which leads to altruistic behavior.[10]

Altruism may be defined as voluntarily helping another in a way that involves a risk or sacrifice to oneself and that does not include any external reward.[11]

Extensivity refers to a wide or extended sense of who is part of one's family, who is one's kin and belongs within one's circle of altruistic care:[12] "What distinguished rescuers was their capacity for extensive relationships—their stronger sense of attachment to others for the welfare of others, including those outside their immediate familial or communal circles."[13] In Doerr's *All the Light We Cannot See*, the Nazis tried to convince Werner that this circle was very small. For rescuers, such as the Danes and Chambonnais, the circle was very large.

When we interviewed SOA Watch founder Roy Bourgeois, he told us how his circle of care expanded. As a young man, he joined the military and served as a naval officer in Vietnam. The violence he saw horrified him. A priest who ran an orphanage for Vietnamese children befriended Roy and took him to visit the orphanage. Besides losing their parents, many of the children had been mutilated by American bombing, including the use of napalm.

One four-year-old girl had lost her sight in one eye, and the other eye was infected. If her blind eye was not removed, she might lose her good eye, too. Roy took the child to a U.S. military doctor, and asked if he could help her. The doctor replied that he could do wonders for her by providing a glass eye and doing skin grafts. However, the doctor refused to treat the child because she was Vietnamese and not U.S. military personnel. Roy was appalled and said, "But we killed her parents when we bombed their village! She lost her eye because of us." Roy's empathy for the wounded Vietnamese child and his altruistic willingness to go out of his way for that child were as great as if the child had been American. Roy had extended his circle of care to include people he had thought of as the "enemy."[14]

As Roy experienced, the three qualities of empathy, altruism, and extensivity reinforced one another and worked together in rescuers on behalf of the Jews. The rescuers empathically felt the Jews' suffering so acutely and saw them as part of their extended human family to such an extent that they felt compelled to risk their own lives to help the Jews. This altruistic response to people in need was so automatic and instinctive that "most rescuers reported rarely reflecting before acting."[15] This is comparable to the Chambonnais who, when interviewed later about their having risked their lives to save so many Jews, said, "It was the human thing to do," meaning they acted on behalf of the Jews without question,[16] as did the Danes who sprang into action on October 1, 1943, to warn their Jews of the Nazis' plans.

Gandhi and Extensivity

Gandhi understood the relationship of extensivity to active non-violence. During the violent conflict between Hindus and Muslims following Indian independence from the British, Gandhi declared a fast and vowed that he would not eat until the killing stopped. In the movie *Gandhi,* as Gandhi lies on his bed a Hindu man bursts in, throws a piece of bread at Gandhi, and the following conversation ensues:

Hindu Man (in a distraught voice): "Eat! I am already going to hell, and I don't want your death on my soul, too."

Gandhi: "Why are you going to hell?"

Hindu man: "Because I killed a child. The Muslims killed my son and so I killed one of their children. I smashed its head against a wall!"

Gandhi: "I know a way out of hell. Find a Muslim boy the same age as your son, whose parents have been killed in this war. Adopt that child and raise him as your own. But be sure you raise him as a Muslim."[17]

We don't know if this literally happened as depicted in the movie, or if it is a dramatization of Gandhi's inclusive attitude toward people on both sides of the Hindu–Muslim conflict.

Gandhi understood that nonviolence requires reaching out very far, even to our enemies, because they are human beings like ourselves. This is the meaning of extensivity.

Other Characteristics of Rescuers

Besides empathy, altruism, and extensivity, another characteristic of rescuers is a sense of internal control and personal efficacy (meaning confidence in one's ability to have an effect on one's environment):[18]

> more than others, rescuers felt that they could control events and shape their own destinies and were more willing to risk failure . . . [they were able to] recognize a choice where others perceived only compliance, and to believe they could succeed where others foresaw only failure.[19]

Related to their sense of personal efficacy, the rescuers also had enough self-esteem to not be intimidated by those in power and to refuse to cooperate with anything that was humiliating. They were, therefore, capable of what Gandhi, Martin Luther King Jr., and Gene Sharp described as the foundation of nonviolent action, which is to withdraw cooperation and obedience from oppressors. Seventeen-year-old Arne Sejr exemplified these qualities of internal control, personal efficacy, and self-esteem, when he wrote his "Ten Commandments for Danes," as did the Native American teenagers who began the relay run to stop the Dakota Access Pipeline, as did the Parkland students when they organized the March for Our Lives.

Additional characteristics of people who engage in active nonviolence are courage, stubbornness in holding to what they believe is right, a universal sense of spirituality, and creativity. This creativity can include thinking outside the box and a sense of humor. Creativity and humor are especially helpful in creating the sense of wonder mentioned earlier (see chapter 7) that is incompatible with cruelty.

Humor: From Moving S-l-o-w-l-y to
Naked Nigerian Women to Wifepower

During the dictatorship of Augusto Pinochet in Chile, a large part of the population used creativity and humor to resist. They agreed that every day at noon everyone from street sweepers to bus drivers to shopkeepers would move v-e-r-y s-l-o-w-l-y. This surprised and bewildered Pinochet's troops. It also established a sense of solidarity among the people that gave them courage to resist in increasingly visible ways, which eventually led to the end of Pinochet's regime.[20]

Another example of creativity and humor is women in Nigeria who were protesting ChevronTexaco's exploitive practices in their community. The women threatened to take off their clothes, because they knew this was a profound cultural taboo that would create "a paralyzing dilemma for the male Nigerian employees," who would be asked to remove the women. The oil company executives backed down and agreed to negotiate the women's demands for fair labor practices and investment in their community.[21]

> Without firing a shot or injuring a soul [the women] shut down an operation that produces a half million barrels of oil a day. In the end, they accomplished what their men could not, and what their government should have done long ago.[22]

In the current environment of white supremacist gatherings, humor may be one of our most valuable nonviolent strategies. In chapter 1, we described how villagers of Wunsiedel, Germany, used humor to turn neo-Nazi demonstrations into fundraisers for EXIT-Germany, an organization that helps people leave violent right-wing groups. EXIT-Germany used humor again at the 2017 "Rock for Germany" music festival in Gera, Germany, an event sponsored by the white supremacist neo-Nazi Democratic Party.

EXIT-German gave nearly three hundred attendees free T-shirts with a skull-and-crossbones logo that said, "Hardcore Rebels—National and Free," a nationalistic message. What the recipients did not know was that when they went home and put their new T-shirts through the washing machine, the original message would fade and a hidden one would appear that said: "If your T-shirt can do it, you can do it, too—we'll help you get away from right-wing extremism." The intention was to use humor to reach young right-wing extremists when they might be home alone and more able to reflect on their situation than when surrounded by other extremists.[23]

In Charlotte, North Carolina, white supremacist members of the National Socialist Movement and the Ku Klux Klan held a rally to promote an anti-immigrant message by speaking out against Charlotte's Latino population. The Latin American Coalition organized a counterdemonstration that used humor to drown out the hatred of the rally. The counterprotestors dressed as clowns, and they parodied the "white power" message of their opponents by holding up "wife power" signs and throwing white flour in the air. One counterprotestor said, "I think it's really important to have a sense of humor. What they want is for us to fight them. They want us to hit them with hate, and we can't become them."[24]

Reflection Process

1. Close your eyes and put your feet flat on the floor. Breathe slowly and deeply. Place your hand on your heart and imagine that you are breathing in and out through your heart.

2. When did you reach out to someone in need, automatically and instinctively, without reflecting before acting? How did you feel afterward?

3. What does this experience tell you about who you really are?

Reflection Questions

What touched me most in this chapter is . . .

When I reflect on this chapter in relation to my life, I feel . . .

I want . . .

Chapter 13

Are Empathy, Altruism, and Extensivity Innate?

No one is born hating another person because of the color of his skin or his background or his religion. People must learn to hate, and if they can learn to hate, they can be taught to love. For love comes more naturally to the human heart than its opposite.

Nelson Mandela[1]

The three main characteristics of those who nonviolently resist oppression on behalf of others are empathy, altruism, and extensivity. Are these characteristics innate to humans?

If we ask this question at a conference, some people raise their hands to say yes, some people raise their hands to say no, and some people move their hands up and down, as if to say they are not sure. Our answer to this question matters, because we tend to behave according to our self-image. If we believe we are kind and caring people, we will be more likely to behave that way.[2]

The Effect of Darwin

Those in Western culture who would answer no to this question about human nature might do so because they have been influenced by a popular interpretation of Charles Darwin's theory of evolution. The words that are commonly attributed to Darwin and associated with his theory are "survival of the fittest." We usually take these words to mean that living creatures are engaged with one another in an often violent struggle for survival, in which the strong survive by conquering the weak. As it turns out, this is a misunderstanding of Darwin.

In his book *The Descent of Man,* Darwin focuses on what drives human development. Evolutionary scientist Dr. David Loye did a word search of *The Descent of Man,* and he found the phrase "survival of the fittest" only once. In that same book, Darwin writes about love ninety-five times and about moral sensitivity ninety-two times. Loye concludes that Darwin believed human evolution is based on the capacity for love, empathy, and moral sensitivity. In other words, the "fittest" are not those who are the most violent but rather those who are the most caring toward others.[3] Darwin's term for empathy is "the social instinct." He saw it as deeply ingrained[4] and as "a powerful aid to survival."[5]

Loye's findings are consistent with "The Seville Statement on Violence," written in 1986 by an international committee of twenty scholars at the Sixth International Colloquium on Brain and Aggression (see the Appendix). This statement was an effort to correct ways in which a misunderstanding of Darwin's theory of evolution has been used to argue that humans are naturally violent and to justify war. The statement was later adopted by UNESCO (United Nations Educational, Scientific and Cultural Organization) and endorsed by scientific organizations around the world, including the Council of Representatives of the American Psychological Association.

Do Soldiers on the Battlefield Want to Kill?

Studies of the behavior of soldiers in war support the Seville Statement. Lieutenant Colonel Dave Grossman, who taught psychology at West Point, has collected research on how soldiers behave on the battlefield. He found that, apart from sociopaths (about 2 to 4 percent of the population in the Western world), who may not feel remorse about killing, the large majority of humans will do whatever they can to avoid killing one another.

Evidence collected from the Battle of Gettysburg through World War II found that 80 or more percent of soldiers would aim their guns high, aim them low, or pretend to be reloading, even when someone from the other side was trying to kill them. The remaining 15 to 20 percent of soldiers (apart from the sociopaths) would shoot to kill, but only because they were under so much pressure to do so.[6]

In 1947, S. L. A. Marshall, a military analyst, who was the chief historian of World War II and who had interviewed hundreds of infantry companies, wrote:

> On average not more than 15% of the men had actually fired at the enemy.... The best showing that could be made by the most spirited and aggressive companies was that one man in four had made at the least some use of his fire power.... These men may face danger but they will not fight.[7]

Psychiatric studies of battle fatigue found that

> fear of killing, rather than fear of being killed, was the most common cause of battle failure in the individual.... It is therefore reasonable to believe that the average and normally healthy individual—the man who can endure the physical and mental stresses of combat—still has such an inner and usually unrealized resistance toward killing a fellow man that he will not of his own volition take life if it is possible to turn away from that responsibility.[8]

The military was very worried about this, and they designed programs to condition soldiers to kill. These programs were so successful that, by the Korean War, the military was able to raise the killing rate from 15 or 20 percent to 65 percent, and by the Vietnam War the killing rate was 90 to 95 percent.[9] Even so, as we mentioned in chapter 4, the Vietnam War was so abhorrent to soldiers that over 500,000 of them deserted.

Moreover, when those soldiers who stayed and fought returned home from Vietnam, large numbers of them suffered from Post-Traumatic Stress Disorder (PTSD), which may lead to suicide. For example, veterans are only 7 percent of the population, but they account for 20 percent of the suicides in the United States.[10] Veterans who killed someone themselves are significantly more likely to suffer from PTSD than those who only observed killing or other atrocities.[11] Killing another human being is so contrary to our nature that when we go against who we really are in this way, we suffer what psychologists who treat PTSD are now calling "moral injury." This is a wound to the soul caused by going against one's conscience.[12]

Two Fathers

I (Sheila) saw this kind of wounding in my own father. He was drafted into the army, and he was badly damaged by his participation in war. He had chronic back pain from a physical injury while he was a soldier. Far worse was the emotional pain he suffered for the rest of his life. Once when I was a child, my father and I were in the shopping area of our town. He suddenly pulled me into the doorway of a store, pointed down the street, and cried out, "There they are! They're coming to get me because of that woman I shot while I was in the army." My father was a basically kind and moral person. He never recovered from going against his own nature by killing another human being.

My (Denny's) father was also a kind and moral person. He was nearly drafted, but he got a deferment because he had fallen arches. He never killed or even seriously harmed anyone. Unlike Sheila's father, he did not suffer moral injury, and I wonder if this is one of the reasons my father lived such a long and happy life.

We Are Hard-Wired for Empathy

Recent neurological and psychological research supports the results of the studies of soldiers on the battlefield. It demonstrates that humans are not naturally violent but rather innately empathic, altruistic, and open to extending their care to a wide range of people. Young children have an inborn sense of what John heard in Hendrik Voss when we interviewed Hendrik about his work with SOA Watch: a sense of kinship with others, of "he is me," of being part of a "we" rather than just an "I."[13] This sense of kinship means we feel what others feel, which is the basis of empathy.

For example, infants as young as one or two days old can recognize when other newborns are crying, and they will cry in return.[14] Babies less than one year old can distinguish kind from unkind behavior toward others, and they indicate a preference for those who behave kindly.[15]

By fourteen months of age, infants will try to help an adult who has a problem. In an experiment with eighteen-month-olds, the researcher did a task in front of the children, such as hanging towels with clothespins or stacking books. Sometimes he would knock over the books or drop the clothespins. Every one of the twenty-four children crawled over to help him pick up the books or the clothespins, but only when his face and body showed that he really needed help. If he deliberately dropped a book or a clothespin, the children did not try to help him. This indicates how sensitively they were attuned to him. The researcher was careful not to reward the children in any way, not even by thanking them. "The toddlers expressed a pure sense of altruism—offering help with no expectation of getting something in return."[16]

Many such experiments with young children have led researchers to conclude that "children's early helping is not a behavior created by culture and/or parental socialization practices. Rather, it is an outward expression of children's natural inclination to sympathize with others in strife."[17] For example,

I (John) don't remember this, but my parents have told me that when I was one year old, we were in the Denver airport and I heard a baby crying. I pointed in the direction of the baby, and said to my mother, "Mama, give John's milk."

Mirror Neurons

Empathy is the first step of the altruistic behavior that John demonstrated at the age of one. The biological basis for empathy is mirror neurons, which were discovered in the 1990s by Giacomo Rizzolatti.[18] Mirror neurons are what allow our brain literally to mirror the brain of another, because the same circuits are activated in our brain that correspond to the circuits that are activated in the other's brain. For instance, if we hear someone cry in anguish (or hunger, as in the case of John in the airport), the mirror neurons in our brain that correspond with our own feelings of anguish are activated, and so we feel the anguish that the other person feels.[19] Mirror neurons are "'What gives you the richness of empathy, the fundamental mechanism that makes seeing someone hurt really hurt you.' . . . The brain acts almost identically when we sense our own feelings and those of another."[20] In other words, we are hardwired for empathy; our brains are programmed for kindness.[21]

Our empathic response, based on mirror neurons, then triggers the motor areas of our brain that prepare us to act on behalf of the person for whom we feel empathy.[22] "To feel *with* stirs us to act *for*," and "the primal brain-to-brain link" makes us want to help anyone—not just those like ourselves.[23] In their studies of prosocial behavior, that is, "any act designed to increase others' well-being," researchers Jamil Zaki and Jason Mitchell found,

> Rather than requiring control over instinctive selfishness, prosocial behavior appears to stem from processes that are intuitive, reflexive, and even automatic . . . prosocial behavior—instead of requiring active control over our impulses—represents an impulse of its own.[24]

In other words, we don't need to control or override selfish impulses in order to help others, because the impulse to help is more instinctive and automatic than selfishness. This matches the reports of the rescuers, the Chambonnais, and the Danes: they acted on behalf of others immediately and without thinking.

Kindness Is Like Chocolate

The consensus of all this research is that humans are born naturally inclined to empathy, altruism, and extensivity, that these are instinctive responses, and that we are happiest when we use these capacities. Scientists at the National Institutes of Health have discovered that "altruistic acts activate a primitive part of the brain, producing a pleasurable response."[25] Or, as Jamil Zaki says, "Kindness and nice behaviors might be psychological chocolate."[26] Even just watching someone else's kindness creates a glowing feeling that psychologists call "elevation" and makes us even more eager to be kind to others.[27]

Kindness Needs the Support of the Environment

Although we are naturally inclined to empathy, altruism, and extensivity, development of these capacities requires the support of the environment, beginning in the womb. If the mother uses drugs or conveys rejection to her baby, the developing neurological pathways for empathy can be damaged.[28] After birth, babies need constant loving physical contact, and whenever a baby is held and responded to empathically, areas of the brain related to love and empathy are stimulated. The more these circuits are stimulated, the more they develop.

When the circuits associated with love and empathy are turned on, the circuits associated with violence are turned off, and do not develop.[29] James Prescott studied forty-nine non-European societies in terms of how much loving touch children experienced and how much violence existed among adults. He found that, in general, societies with more loving touch had less violence, and societies with less loving touch had more violence.[30]

Beginning in the mid-twentieth century, psychologists who studied child development began to see the desire for connection and companionship as fundamental to humans and as the core of human nature.[31] Pioneers in this field, such as John Bowlby and Mary Ainsworth, realized that what babies and developing children most need is a secure attachment to a primary caregiver, who is constantly and empathically present to them.[32] Securely attached children have a highly developed capacity for empathy. As psychologist L. Alan Sroufe said,

> How do you get an empathetic child? You get an empathetic child not by trying to teach the child and admonish the child to be empathic, you get an empathic child by being empathic with the child. The child's understanding of relationships can only be from relationships he's experienced.[33]

The studies of rescuers are consistent with this research. The Oliners found that

> strong and cohesive family bonds were the primary source of their psychological strength and values. Above all, these rescuers perceived their relationships with their families of origin as very close. They felt strongly attached to their fathers as well as their mothers.[34]

This secure early attachment resulted in trust, security, curiosity, and self-directedness. Because their relationship with their parents was so satisfying, and because their parents emphasized the importance of caring relationships, the rescuers were open to relating to a wide range of people in a caring way.

The threat of punishment inhibits caring behavior.[35] Gandhi understood this and said, "Power is of two kinds. One is obtained by fear of punishment, and the other by acts of love.

Power based on love is a thousand times more effective and per-
manent than the one derived from fear of punishment."[36] Most
rescuers were never physically punished as children. Instead,
their parents guided them by helping them understand the
effect of their behavior on others (what is called "inductive
reasoning"), and by their own example of caring behavior.[37] In
other words, rescuers were consistently treated with love and
empathy by their parents, and this became the rescuers' consistent response to all other people.

In contrast, a study of juvenile offenders found that the most
violent ones came from violent homes. Seventy percent had
seen extreme violence in their homes, and 75 percent had been
physically abused by parents.[38] Psychologist Heinz Kohut concluded that human destructiveness comes from the frustration
of the child's need for empathic responses: "'Aggression . . . as a
psychological phenomenon is not elemental.' . . . If the empathic
response of the parent is weak or nonexistent, the child's development is arrested . . . and destructive rage sets in."[39]

However, when our basic needs, especially for empathy and
care, are met, we naturally and instinctively reach out to a wide
range of others with empathy and care, especially those in need.
In chapter 8, we wondered why the Poles collaborated with the
Nazis to kill Jews while the Danes resisted the Nazis in order to
save their Jews. Could it be that differences in parenting practices a century or so ago between Poland and Denmark made
the difference? Were the needs for empathy and care of Danish
children who grew up to save Jews met, while the same needs
of Polish children who grew up to collaborate in killing Jews
were not met? Maybe someday I (John) will research this as a
graduate school project.

Kitty Genovese and the Milgram Experiment

Even humans who have been raised to be kind do not always
behave that way. For most of us, the qualities of empathy, altru-

ism, and extensivity require the support of not only the home environment but the larger world as well. This is illustrated by a famous story of violence and a famous experiment.

The story, as reported in the *New York Times* on March 13, 1964, is that of Kitty Genovese, a young woman living in Queens. A killer stalked and stabbed her repeatedly. At least thirty-eight people saw the attack and/or heard her screams. Not one of them called the police during the assault, and only one person called the police after she was dead.[40]

The experiment, known as "The Milgram Experiment," was first performed by social psychologist Dr. Stanley Milgram in 1963. Repeated variations of this experiment demonstrated that 61 to 66 percent of participants will administer what they believe to be painful electric shocks to subjects simply because the subject paired words incorrectly when directed to do so by an authority figure. Significantly, only 10 percent of participants will administer the shocks if at least two other participants refuse to do so.[41]

These examples of human beings *not* demonstrating empathy, altruism, or extensivity reveal how vulnerable we are to authority figures and to our social environment. For example, note the difference in the number of participants willing to administer electric shock in the Milgram Experiment when only two others refused to do so: 10 percent vs. 61 to 66 percent. What if just two people had called the police while Kitty Genovese was being attacked? What if only one person had cried out, "Let's go help her!" Perhaps the other bystanders would have remembered their innate desire to care for those in need as well, and rushed to her aid.

Blue Eyes/Brown Eyes[42]

One of the most graphic illustrations of how much our environment can affect our ability to express empathy, altruism, and extensivity is a classic social science experiment known as

"Blue Eyes/Brown Eyes." This originated with Jane Elliott, a third-grade teacher in a small town in Iowa in the 1960s, where everyone was white and Christian.[43]

After the assassination of Martin Luther King, Jane wanted a way to help her third-graders understand prejudice. So, she devised an experiment. She began class one day by telling her students,

> Today, the blue-eyed people will be on the bottom and the brown-eyed people on the top. What I mean is that brown-eyed people are better than blue-eyed people. They are cleaner than blue-eyed people. They are more civilized than blue-eyed people. And they are smarter than blue-eyed people.[44]

She told the brown-eyed children that only they could have five extra minutes at recess, use the big playground equipment, go first to lunch and return for second helpings. And, Jane said, "Blue-eyed people are not allowed to play with brown-eyed people unless they are invited." She instructed the blue-eyed children to sit in the back of the room, and gave each brown-eyed child a collar to put on a blue-eyed child.

Throughout the day, every time a brown-eyed child got the right answer in class or did almost anything, Jane would say, "See! Brown-eyed children are smart and they do things right." Every time a blue-eyed child made a mistake, she would say, "What do you expect?! That's just how blue-eyed children are!" By lunchtime, it was obvious whether a child was blue- or brown-eyed:

> The brown-eyed children were happy, alert, having the time of their lives. And they were doing far better work than they had ever done before. The blue-eyed children were miserable. Their posture, their expressions, their entire attitudes were those of defeat. Their classroom work regressed sharply from that of the day before. Inside of an hour or so, they looked and acted as if they were, in fact, inferior. It was shocking.

But even more frightening was the way the brown-eyed children turned on their friends of the day before. . . .[45]

The next day, Jane reversed the experiment, and this time she labeled the blue-eyed ones as superior. The same thing happened in reverse. At the end of the day, she told the children it was only an experiment and there was no innate difference between blue-eyed and brown-eyed people. The children took off their collars and hugged one another, looking immensely relieved to be equals and friends again. In other words, in an environment of inclusive love, they recovered their innate capacity for empathy, altruism, and extensivity.

Like Jane's students, except for an exceptionally courageous few of us, we require a supportive environment in order to fully express this innate capacity. The Danes and the Chambonnais provided this supportive environment for one another, including trusted leaders (such as King Christian X and André Trocmé) who modeled care for everyone. The Polish rescuers of Jews did not have a supportive larger social environment, but their original, family environment was very supportive of empathic behavior. Moreover, they were parented in ways that helped them develop a strong enough sense of inner authority to resist negative social pressure.

Nonviolence Is Natural

After many years of organizing farm workers to resist injustice, Cesar Chavez said, "I think nonviolence is a very natural way of doing things, and violence is highly out of the ordinary."[46] In other words, to be truly human is to be nonviolent. The research we have cited, on rescuers and on neurological and psychological development, demonstrates that when humans are able to grow in an environment that supports our innate tendencies, we are empathic, altruistic, and extensive, all of which lead to nonviolence. Given our susceptibility to the social environment that surrounds us, how can we foster an environment that supports these tendencies, as well as the courage to resist authority that asks us to do otherwise?

Reflection Process

1. Close your eyes and put your feet flat on the floor. Breathe slowly and deeply. Place your hand on your heart and imagine that you are breathing in and out through your heart.

2. How does the environment in which you now live support empathy, altruism, and extensivity? How does your environment undermine or discourage these qualities?

3. As you continue to breathe in and out through your heart, breathe into yourself the ways your environment supports empathy, altruism, and extensivity. Let those qualities grow in your heart. Breathe them out into whatever aspects of your environment do not support them. Imagine those aspects of your environment changing to become kinder and more caring.

Reflection Questions

What touched me most in this chapter is . . .

When I reflect on this chapter in relation to my life, I feel . . . I want . . .

Chapter 14

Fostering Active Nonviolence

Speaking of the natural capacity for nonviolence that we all possess, Michael Nagler writes,

> *Most of us don't try to develop it, for the simple reason we don't know we have it. But that is due to our cultural conditioning. . . . The conditioning is secondary, and can therefore be dislodged relatively easily: last in, first out. The biggest problem with civilization as we know it is that it has somehow taken the shadow for the light. I think, in fact, that it's violence that's artificial.*[1]

Since the capacity for nonviolence is natural to human beings, anything that fosters healthy human development fosters nonviolence, beginning with nourishing food, exposure to nature, exercise, and clean air. Most of all, human beings need an environment of love. As emphasized in chapter 13, the beginning of healthy human development and the best way to foster nonviolence is parenting that emphasizes attachment and empathy.

Schools have an important role to play, as well, by creating a loving environment, where everyone feels safe and cared for. A program that exemplifies this and that has been used in many schools is "Roots of Empathy," developed by Mary Gordon.[2] The real teachers in this program are babies. A mother with a new baby will visit a class of students, perhaps as young as eight or nine, several times over a period of months. The students observe the baby as it develops and watch it closely, empathically attuning themselves to how the baby is feeling and what it needs.

More than 800,000 schoolchildren thus far have participated in the Roots of Empathy program. A study of a large number of them found an 88 percent drop in "proactive aggression," that is, the use of aggression in a cold-hearted manner to get what you want.[3] Mary Gordon understands that early attachment is the foundation of caring behavior toward others, that attachment fosters empathy, and that children can still learn empathy if they have not gotten enough of it at home.

Significantly, Roots of Empathy involves groups of children observing empathic behavior in one another. This may help them develop the courage to resist social pressure to tolerate cruelty, as in the case of those who walked right by Kitty Genovese, or to participate in cruelty themselves by administering electric shocks, as in Stanley Milgram's experiment (see chapter 13).

Roots of Empathy is only one of many programs and styles of education that schools can use to bring out children's innate empathy, altruism, and extensivity. Other programs include social-emotional learning (SEL) programs; collaborative learning, where students work together and help one another learn; cross-age contact, where older students care for younger ones; programs that encourage social awareness and diversity, such as international student programs; and service programs that provide ways to reach out to those in need and learn from them. All of this might be enough to produce nonviolent people, if it were not for the fact that we are immersed in a violent culture.

Our Culture Discourages Empathy and Encourages Violence

Neuroscientist Marco Iacoboni suggests that "externally manipulated, massive belief systems, including political ideologies, tend to override the unconscious, pre-reflective, neurobiological traits that should bring us together."[4] American culture is based on belief systems that discourage empathy and encourage violence in many ways.

First of all, our culture teaches us that we are separate from one another and, even more, that we must compete with one another to succeed. We are pitted against one another in most aspects of life, including grades in school, educational testing, college admissions, sports, and who gets the best of a diminishing number of good jobs.

Our culture also offers us constant distractions from being present to one another, such as technological gadgets. These devices can be used for great good and have been instrumental in recent social justice movements, including the #NeverAgain movement. Without cell phones and social media, the Parkland students could never have organized a vast and worldwide network of supporters, marches, walkouts, and rallies in just a few short weeks, nor could they continue to hold the movement together.

However, these devices can also disconnect us from ourselves and from being empathically present to others. I (John) have observed my friends, sitting in the same room or even next to each other, texting one another rather than making eye contact and talking. In fact, "talking" often doesn't even mean saying words to another person any more. Rather, it can mean messaging back and forth on Facebook or texting. Adults often tell me and my parents how much they appreciate the way I make eye contact and appear to be empathically present to them. Although I am not aware of doing anything unusual, I think what they are observing is the result of my not having had a cell phone for most of my life.

I have one now, because I need it for college. I see how tempting it is to check my phone often for messages and how distracting this can be. I have tried to learn about the risks of having a phone, in hopes that I can avoid them and maintain my capacity for human connection and empathic presence. I learned that the "twin rise of the smartphone and social media has caused an earthquake of a magnitude we've not seen in a very long time, if ever" in the associated increased rate of teenage suicide, loneliness, and depression.[5]

These effects of phones and other devices are related to the biochemistry of addiction. The average owner of a cell phone checks it about nine times every hour, or 110 times a day. Like sugar and other addictive substances and processes, checking a phone gives a kind of "high" that releases dopamine in the brain. The high wears off quickly, and we want another "hit" to get another dopamine high. However, dopamine depletes serotonin, and it is serotonin that gives us a lasting feeling of happiness.[6] No wonder teens who habitually use phones are depressed. As one lonely teen reflected, "We didn't have a choice to know any life without iPads or iPhones. I think we like our phones more than we like actual people."[7]

I like actual people, but when phones and other devices are constantly nearby, I am tempted to use them, and my attention is divided. This means my brain "must shift focus between two, three, or four things, and there are 'switching costs' including lessened cognitive abilities, mental fatigue and *reduced empathy*."[8] As psychologist Dr. Daniel Goleman, known for his work on emotional intelligence, says, if kids "don't build up the neural circuitry that focused attention requires, they could have problems controlling their emotions and being empathetic."[9] I hope my neural circuitry for focused attention on other human beings is developed enough that my new phone won't take over my life!

Fortunately, even for kids who grew up having electronic devices and suffer their effects, these effects can be reversed. A study done at UCLA involved sixth-graders who spent a week at an outdoor camp, away from all electronic devices and in face-to-face contact with other people. They became significantly more able to accurately identify the emotions on others' faces than a group of their peers who stayed home and followed their usual routine of screen time.[10]

Screens not only diminish empathy by removing us from direct human contact, but they also expose us to images and messages that diminish empathy and encourage violence. In the previous chapter, we mentioned the intentional desensitization of soldiers to violence, so they would be willing to kill. Although most of us are not preparing for the battlefield, our culture desensitizes us to violence by repeatedly exposing us to it through TV, movies, and violent video games. These games are marketed to children and designed to encourage them to join the military.[11] All of this makes children fearful and aggressive and desensitizes them to killing.[12]

Another way our culture encourages violence is by choosing violence as a solution to problems. The "mass shooting generation" has not only spent their entire lives wondering if their school would be next; they have also spent their lives in a country that has been constantly at war around the world and that promotes militarism at home. From proposals to prevent school shootings by arming teachers to increasingly militarized police forces, we encourage violence. How can we expect insecure, impressionable people in our country to stop blowing one another up with guns while we as a nation encourage them to believe that killing makes us strong, and we celebrate blowing people up in other parts of the world? As psychiatrist Dr. Alexander Bukhanovsky said, "Giant militarized countries breed violent populations."[13]

This celebration of violence is reflected in how history is typically taught, in terms of who won or lost wars, rather than in terms of successful nonviolent campaigns. As Michael Nagler says, "Every time we use violence to solve a problem we send the signal that violence is the way to solve problems,"[14] and as John Dear writes,

> We have all experienced violence. We have all suffered violence. We are taught violence is normal; the way of the world, the way of life. . . . We're all brainwashed into violence. We have learned well how to be violent. We now have to unlearn those lessons and learn how to be nonviolent. We need to be trained in nonviolence.[15]

Unlearning Violence

Fortunately, unlearning violence may not be all that difficult. In an experiment done in 1951 with forty children ages seven to nine, half of them were trained in cooperative behavior. This included drawing murals and completing jigsaw puzzles. All aggressive behavior was discouraged, and constructive behavior was encouraged. The other half were trained in a way that encouraged the aggressive tendencies they already had. (An experiment encouraging aggression would likely be considered unethical today.) For example, the children played games in which the goal was to injure some object or person.

All the children were then put in a highly frustrating situation, and they were observed by the researchers. The children whose aggressive tendencies had been encouraged engaged in fights, arguments, and other destructive behavior more than ever. However, those who had been trained in cooperative behavior were more cooperative than ever. Michael Nagler's interpretation of this is that the training in cooperation seemed to create a kind of energy channel, and when the frustration occurred, the energy of it flowed through that channel and was expressed as cooperation.[16] Nagler concludes, "Peace could be a simple matter of training."[17]

Scientific research on neuroplasticity (meaning the brain's ability to change and to produce new neurons throughout life) demonstrates that "any form of training leads to a reconfiguring in the brain on both the functional and structural levels."[18] This means that not only children but also adults who have been immersed in violence and are then put into an environment of empathy and altruism can grow new neurons that support nonviolence.

John Dear tells the following story:

> I had an 85-year-old nun friend who did six months hard time, for crossing the line at the SOA [School of the Americas]. . . . She was put in this cell, as punishment by

the judge, who hated this old nun so much he put her in the one cell in the U.S. with serial mass murder women. So, here's this nun in a cell that you never leave, with six women who killed over ten people each. And, in ten minutes, she had them all in the palm of her hand, and she loved them and she changed all their lives. She healed them. This is how nonviolence works—you just be human with the other person. You just show kindness, and they had never seen kindness before, much less met a great person like my friend Sr. Sheila.[19]

Reflection Process

1. Close your eyes and put your feet flat on the floor. Breathe slowly and deeply. Place your hand on your heart and imagine that you are breathing in and out through your heart.

2. When have you been in the presence of an utterly kind and loving person, someone whose kindness was so great that you felt entirely safe? How did it affect you to be with this person? How were you changed by this experience?

3. As you continue to breathe in and out through your heart, breathe into yourself the safety and love you felt with this person, and let it grow in your heart. You carry this person with you forever.

Reflection Questions

What touched me most in this chapter is . . .

When I reflect on this chapter in relation to my life, I feel . . .

I want . . .

Chapter 15

Is It Possible to Stop
Violence in Its Path?

*If every 8 year old in the world is taught meditation, we will
eliminate violence from the world within one generation.*

The Dalai Lama[1]

One of the reviewers who read the manuscript for this book is
Malia Barca, an especially thoughtful young woman and John's
close friend since they were both three years old. She asked an
important question in response to what we have said about
nonviolence being natural when we remember who we are. In
her comments to us, she wrote:

> How can a large group of perhaps frightened and angry
> people be reminded "of who they are"? How can we "get
> through" to the angry, especially when anger and fear
> often cause impulsivity and irrationality? In my experi-
> ence, frightened and angry people are the most likely to
> act violently, and they are also the least likely to take the
> time to listen to logic or reason. Many of today's issues
> seem to be so large scale and already so far out of hand,
> that I have difficulty wrapping my head around the idea
> that a large group of people already on the path to vio-
> lent action could be persuaded to take nonviolent action
> instead. Is it possible to stop violence in its path? Or is the
> only option to cut violence off before it even begins?[2]

Malia's question raises one of the most critical issues of our time. Once violence gets going, especially on a mass scale, it is very difficult to stop. As we wrote in chapter 11, "the longer violence has been allowed to go on unchecked, the more 'soul force' and sacrifice it will take to stop it."

In this book we have offered many examples of seemingly hopeless situations in which violence was stopped. Yet, given the extent of violence in our world, a thorough answer to Malia's question is the work of countless nonviolence researchers and activists, peace institutes, humanitarian organizations, the United Nations, and so forth. To address the problem of violence on a large scale, we would need a national and worldwide commitment to finding nonviolent ways to resolve conflict. We would also need the kind of "soul force" and moral leadership provided by courageous men and women such as Gandhi, King Christian X of Denmark, André and Magda Trocmé in Le Chambon, Martin Luther King Jr., Roy Bourgeois, John Dear, our friend Andrea in Guatemala, David Hogg, Emma Gonzalez, and other student leaders. One reason we wrote this book is our hope that many readers will be inspired to provide this kind of leadership on a small or large scale and contribute to the work of finding alternatives to violence. Meanwhile, a simple answer to Malia's question may already be available to everyone.

Take Two Steps Back and Breathe

When I (John) presented my senior project at Vail Mountain School, Travis Aldrich (the upper school director and my basketball coach) asked me what I would do in a sports situation when I wanted to respond angrily. Without thinking, I said, "Take two steps back and breathe." My answer was better than I realized at the time: A widely used and well-researched way to change the brain in the direction of nonviolence is through breathing, especially when combined with meditation.

For example, research at the Institute of HeartMath has

demonstrated that holding a feeling of appreciation in our heart for as little as ten seconds while breathing deeply can change our heart rhythm from incoherent (erratic and jagged) to coherent (slow and regular, with a wavy rhythm). Our calm heart rhythm then entrains our brain, so that we experience not only more positive emotions, but we think more positive thoughts, as well. Moreover, when our heart rhythm is coherent, we "pull" the heart rates of those around us into coherence.[3] This would be a simple way for any group, including a large group of demonstrators, to remain centered in nonviolence.

Breathing alone, even without finding and holding a feeling of appreciation, has a similarly centering and calming effect. For example, veterans with PTSD are taught a simple breathing process that relieves symptoms of anxiety.[4] A wide variety of groups, institutions, and organizations—from Google to people helping kids with behavior problems—are using breathing to help people relax and get centered in a peaceful inner place. When we are centered in this way, solutions that are based on a nonviolent sense of kinship come naturally.[5] Meditation (which often includes deep breathing) has a similar effect.

In 1993, physicist Dr. John Hagelin designed an experiment to see if meditation could reduce the crime rate in Washington, DC. Crime can be predicted quite accurately three months in advance, by considering factors such as previous crime rate, temperature, day of the week, and so forth. Hagelin proposed to lower the predicted crime rate by at least 20 percent.

He received a $6 million grant for his experiment, and used much of it to bring four thousand experienced meditators from eighty different countries to Washington. During a two-month period, they meditated regularly with the intention that stress and other factors contributing to crime be lowered. In fact, the crime rate diminished by 25 percent. The odds of this being due to chance were less than one in one billion. An independent review board of twenty-seven sociologists, criminologists, etc., verified these results.

During the war in Yugoslavia, Hagelin met with representatives of our National Security Council to say, in light of his
research, "There *is* another way to handle this besides dropping
bombs on Belgrade." He reports that people in our government were well aware of the power of intention to affect world
events, but at the time the vested interests in military solutions
were already too great to be stopped.[6]

Many subsequent studies of meditation have confirmed its
power to affect not only the person practicing it but also the
surrounding environment. At the individual level, for example,
research demonstrated that one person meditating in a room had
a positive effect on another person taking a test in an adjacent
room. The test takers did better on the test, even though they
were unaware of the meditators.[7] Meditation can have the same
effect on negative aspects of the larger social environment, such
as war, sickness, and hunger; it can replace them with positive
qualities, such as peace and understanding. If even just 1 percent
of the population of a city practices meditation, this brings down
the crime rate, the number of missed days of work caused by ill-
ness, and the number of traffic accidents.[8]

John Hagelin explains the effect of meditation on the larger
social environment in terms of a basic principle of nature, which
is that incoherent systems can easily be penetrated by external
influences that are disruptive and disordered, whereas coherent
systems dispel these influences. Meditation creates coherence.
When a large group meditates, that creates coherence on a scale
that cannot be penetrated by negative outside forces and creates
"an effective 'virtual fence' against terrorism."[9] Although the
people of Le Chambon would likely not have heard of meditation, they were united in a prayerful state of coherence. That may
be how they created a "virtual fence" around their town and their
Jewish guests, and stopped the violence of the Nazis in its path.

Reflecting on the studies of meditation to change our social
environment, Dr. David Edwards, a professor of government,
says,

I think the claim can be plausibly made that the potential impact of this research exceeds that of any other ongoing social or psychological research program. It has survived a broader array of statistical tests than most research in the field on conflict resolution. This work and the theory that informs it deserve the most serious consideration by academics and policymakers alike.[10]

Breathing and meditation are ways to reverse the cultural conditioning of violence taught by our culture and to remember who we are by growing new neurons that support nonviolence. Dr. Marco Iacoboni, known for his work on mirror neurons, says that we are so "wired for empathy" that if we stopped all the artificial violence around us for even just one week, it would make such a difference that the level of violence in our culture could be brought down to very minimal levels and we would be on our way to living in a nonviolent culture.[11]

Meanwhile, we can all begin with ourselves. Based on our current understanding of neuroplasticity, studies of meditation, and the research of the HeartMath Institute, we can each find the resources to heal fear and anger within ourselves as we remember who we are, and we can help our friends and neighbors to do the same.

Remembering Who We Are

If you would like to try it, following is a simple, meditative breathing process that we do at the end of every day:

1. Close your eyes, put your feet flat on the floor and breathe deeply. Place your hand on your heart and imagine that you are breathing in and out through your heart.

2. Bring to your heart a positive memory of a time when you experienced gratitude and love, from today or from any time in your life. Hold your feeling of appreciation for that moment in your heart for a while, and relive the parts that move you most. Let your feeling of appreciation grow.

3. Be aware that moments of gratitude and love are reminders to you of who you really are.

Reflection Questions

What touched me most in this chapter is . . .
When I reflect on this chapter in relation to my life, I feel . . .
I want . . .

Chapter 16

Personal Reflection: How Nonviolence Was Fostered in Me

Rescuers . . . were and are "ordinary" people. . . . [They] remind us that such courage is available to all through the virtues of connectedness, commitment, and the quality of relationships developed in ordinary human interactions.

Samuel and Pearl Oliner[1]

Although, like all other Americans, I (John) grew up in a culture of violence, I don't believe violence is natural. I know it is not natural to me. I am an ordinary person. I am not perfect, but I experience myself as basically grounded in nonviolence and committed to living a nonviolent life. I have been this way since early childhood.

Whenever we drive by a park in a nearby town, my father reminds me of something that happened there when I was three. Another boy my age, but about half my size, came up and shoved me. My father was surprised that I didn't just flatten the kid. Instead, I walked away and played with some other children. The same boy came up to me and shoved me again. Once more, instead of hitting back, I just walked away. I wasn't afraid of the boy; I just didn't want to hurt him.

About ten years later, once again a boy who was smaller started bullying me. He threw basketballs at my head, pushed me, cut in front of me in lines, and said cruel things to me in front of other kids. This went on for three years. Coaches and other kids who observed this told me and my parents that I was not doing anything to provoke the boy's behavior.

Adults, including my parents, tried to intervene, but the dynamics of the situation were complicated, and the boy's behavior continued. With my parents' support, I tried to find ways to protect myself and maintain my self-respect without striking back. Once I pinned the bully against a wall to stop him from hitting me, but I did not hit him myself. I kept reaching out to this boy, and eventually I was able to connect with him. We are now good friends. I learned from this experience that I am capable of getting angry and wanting to punch somebody, but if I take a couple of steps back and breathe, I become aware that what I most want is a nonviolent solution.

I have as many faults as anyone my age and as much to learn. But I do identify with the long history of nonviolence that we have summarized here, and I want to be like its heroes. How was nonviolence fostered in me? How did I get this way? I believe it is because I was raised in a manner similar to the rescuers as described in the Oliners' research, in an environment of trust, love, and care for the larger community.

Attachment

I was very securely attached to my parents. They held me or carried me in a sling all the time when I was a baby, until I wanted to get down and crawl. Thus, I was in constant loving physical contact with my parents or another caring adult. My mother breast-fed me until I was almost two and a half. Besides my parents, I was surrounded by a community of loving people. Thus, as discussed in chapter 13, the areas of my brain related to love and empathy were stimulated, and the circuits associated with violence were turned off.

If I made a mistake, my parents used reasoning to help me understand the effect of my behavior on myself and others. I was neither punished nor rewarded, and my parents never emphasized obedience. Because I was not punished, I did not learn that more powerful people have the right to hurt less powerful people, and I did not learn to feel powerless or afraid in relation to authorities.

My parents' response to me was nearly always empathetic, and they encouraged me to have and express my feelings. For example, if I fell and hurt myself and started to cry, often other people would say, "Don't cry, you're ok." Or, if we were in Latin America, they would say, "*No es nada*," meaning, "It's nothing." But my parents would say, "It hurts, doesn't it?" Thus, I learned that it was ok for me to cry and show weakness, and so I can let others be weak rather than despising them for it.

Play

I was home schooled until ninth grade, in part because my parents wanted me to have the time and freedom to explore and play. They played with me a lot, as did other adults, and lots of children. We had a big basket full of costumes, most of which my mother made to my specifications. When I wore them, I imagined myself as many different people, and I think this helped me learn to walk in the shoes of others.

My family used play to help me imagine alternatives to violence. For example, when I was six, we began a monthly ritual based on the People Power Revolution in the Philippines. A friend had invited me on an outing with her children, and we stopped at a fast-food restaurant. My meal came with some small plastic toys, including a tank. My parents had never given me weapons, and we never went to places that gave them away. So, we had a family meeting to decide what to do with the tank. One or another of us had an idea: My parents had often told me about the People Power Revolution. We decided we would put the tank away and take it out only on the 26th of each month (the revolution was on February 26, 1986), to act out the revolution. I was in charge, and I could tell each person what role to play. One thing I especially loved about this ritual was that I also got to decide what we would have for dinner that night to celebrate People Power . . . usually homemade burgers and fries.

A Big World

Being home schooled meant that I was allowed to pursue what I was interested in and learn it. I think this helped me develop a strong sense of self. I read all kinds of books, alone or with my mother. I especially loved the novels of Charles Dickens, John Steinbeck, Mark Twain, Frances Hodgson Burnett, and J. K. Rowling. The characters in these novels are still almost as alive to me today as if they were real people. I have since learned that novels that emphasize character development encourage the reader to imagine what it is like to be inside others and thereby foster the growth of empathy in the reader.[2] I believe that is what happened to me.

While we were home schooling, people often asked my parents, "How will John ever get socialized?!," as if they thought the only possible form of socialization was to be in a class of twenty or thirty other kids the same age as me. What actually happened is that home schooling gave me the opportunity to connect with other people of all ages, through play groups, sports teams, and classes in dance, horseback riding, art, pottery, gymnastics, theater, and singing. I was willing to try almost anything, and sometimes I was the only boy in a dance class full of girls. This helped me feel as at home with girls as with boys, and so I was not at the mercy of how boys in our culture are typically socialized, to be tough and aggressive.

Besides participating in a wide range of activities with other children, I also attended grown-up conferences with my parents. Perhaps this is why I have always been entirely comfortable with adults. I think that not owning a cell phone helped me relate directly to all these people, rather than substituting electronic devices for human contact. I did get a computer when I began ninth grade because I needed it for school, and I still struggle with not getting distracted or consumed by it . . . all those sites with sports scores are really tempting!

By the time I began high school, my parents and I had traveled together to forty-eight states and twenty-two countries, and I had learned to relate as an equal to a wide range of people of all social classes and ethnic backgrounds. For example, we have gone to Mexico many times to give conferences, and we have often stayed at a place by the ocean owned by a friend. When I was seven, I volunteered to help out at the restaurant there, as a waiter. For ten years now, I have spent some time most winters at that restaurant working alongside poor Mexicans, serving food and clearing dirty dishes. They have become family friends. I know what life is like for them, as well as I know what it is like for the wealthy or middle-class Mexicans who typically organize our conferences, some of whom are also family friends.

Reaching Out

My parents modeled extensivity by reaching out to care for anyone who needed help. I learned to give just because it feels good, and not in order to get anything in return. We often participated in nonviolent demonstrations or other social justice actions. When I was seven, I started volunteering for political campaigns with my family to elect the candidates we believed would do the most good. All of this taught me to speak up and join others to act on behalf of what I believe is right. The religious teaching in my home was never about religion. Rather it was about universal love and what the Oliners call "the common humanity of all people."[3]

When I started high school at Vail Mountain School (VMS), I fit right in because the school environment was so much like the way I was raised. I especially appreciated the emphasis at VMS on community and social ethics, and how the faculty and staff are always available to interact with students and model what they teach. The school, which is K–12, emphasizes regular contact with younger children. For example, every senior has a "kindergarten buddy."

Classes encourage cooperative learning. Students are not ranked according to their GPA, and no one is chosen as valedictorian. This may be why my classmates were so ready and willing to help one another, and my favorite projects were the ones I worked on with other students. One thing I especially liked at VMS—and that was my biggest problem—was all the service opportunities. I would have gone to the soup kitchen or Habitat for Humanity every day if it were not for classes, homework, sports practice, theater rehearsal, etc., etc.!

In our culture, competition can contribute to violence when it encourages winning at all costs. At many schools, the emphasis on winning means that only the most talented players are chosen for sports teams. At VMS, anyone who wants to play is automatically on a team.

Sports are really important to me, and even though my teams at VMS liked to win, my coaches always made it clear that the welfare of the players matters more than winning. In a video about the VMS athletic field, soccer coach Bob Bandoni expresses the attitude toward sports that I experienced during my years at VMS:

> There's a Hemingway quote we refer to that speaks to being better than our previous self, and we embrace that every day on this field. In a very real way, that is the foundation of good education: an understanding of your responsibility as an individual and how that relates to society, to contributing to something bigger than yourself. This really is about the development of character, it's about the development of community. The games fade, but what we take away from this field stays with us the rest of our lives.[4]

When I played on that field, and now when I watch younger students play there, I see the log cabin above it that houses the Students Shoulder-to-Shoulder program founded by Mr. Bandoni. This program matches groups of students with NGOs in other parts of the world, and organizes service projects for the students. My participation with Students Shoulder-to-Shoulder added immensely to my experience at VMS. I helped build an ecotourism center on a rural island in Cambodia, played with children at a home for AIDS orphans in Kenya, and worked with Lakota kids my age digging holes for fence posts on the Pine Ridge Lakota Sioux Reservation in South Dakota.

When my parents and I went to support the water protectors at Standing Rock, North Dakota, in 2016, I felt that I already knew those people and was part of them because of my experience at Pine Ridge. Every Students Shoulder-to-Shoulder program that I participated in deepened the empathy, altruism, and extensivity that I learned at home and at VMS, and gave me the opportunity to live those qualities with a wide range of people.

I believe that all these aspects of my life have supported the capacity for nonviolence with which I, like all other humans, was born. I don't know if I would have the courage to hide Jews from the Nazis or walk with Gandhi to the sea to make salt or march with the children in Birmingham, but I hope I would.

Reflection Process

1. Close your eyes and put your feet flat on the floor. Breathe slowly and deeply. Place your hand on your heart and imagine that you are breathing in and out through your heart.

2. How did the environment in which you were raised support empathy, altruism, and extensivity? How did your environment undermine or discourage these qualities?

3. As you continue to breathe in and out through your heart, breathe into yourself the ways your home environment supported empathy, altruism, and extensivity. Let those qualities grow in your heart.

Reflection Questions

What touched me most in this chapter is . . .

When I reflect on this chapter in relation to my life, I feel . . .

I want . . .

Stories of Hope

Violence leads to cultural insanity; nonviolence leads to sanity. Nonviolence is the only method that can be used to get a non-violent outcome. . . . War never brings peace. It always sows the seeds for future war.

John Dear[1]

The arc of the moral universe is long, but it bends toward justice.
Martin Luther King Jr.[2]

When I (John) began the senior project that inspired my parents and me to write this book, I wanted to do it because I don't like violence. I feel encouraged by stories of active nonviolence and by my experience of participating in such actions myself. I have learned that not only is nonviolence natural to me, but that it is innate to all humans. Even though we live in a culture of violence that includes racism, sexism, bullying, shootings, and war, we can learn a new way of being based on peace. We have also learned from the research of Erica Chenoweth and Maria Stephan that nonviolence is not just a nice idea that sometimes works, but that it is actually far more effective than violence. It is, as Gandhi said, "the greatest and most active force in the world."

The three of us now accept what John Dear, our friend and cheerleader for this book and one of the greatest living peace activists, says is the bottom line for anyone who believes in nonviolence:

There is no cause for which we will ever again support the taking of a single human life, much less thousands or millions. Jesus, Gandhi, and Martin Luther, King, Jr. share a boundary line: we do not use violence on any other human being ever again. We don't kill people who kill people to show people that killing people is wrong. Instead, we give our lives to stop the killings, join the global, grassroots movement of nonviolence, and work for a new culture of peace and nonviolence.[3]

Consistent with his words, John helped write the pope's message for the January 1, 2017, World Day of Peace, entitled "Nonviolence." It is the first official statement on nonviolence in the history of the Catholic Church.[4]

Then, in April 2019, a conference on nonviolence was held at the Vatican, organized under the leadership of Marie Dennis, copresident of Pax Christi International, and the Vatican Nonviolence Initiative. This and an earlier conference in 2016 are the first times in the history of the Catholic Church that there have been high-level meetings and conferences on nonviolence. For over five years, conference organizers have been in dialogue with the Vatican and Pope Francis about the possibility of a new encyclical on nonviolence. Such an encyclical would have global implications for all churches on all issues of violence and could reverse 1,700 years of just war theory (see page 31). Conference participants cited the effectiveness of nonviolent campaigns that make war outdated, and declared in their final statement, "There is no 'just war.'"[5]

Long before the Vatican caught on, Gandhi claimed that the power of nonviolence was so great that it could be used to eliminate war entirely.[6] We believe this is possible and that nonviolence is and must be the future of our world. We see many recent examples of this that are signs of hope. Because hearing about stories of goodness and kindness activates those qualities in ourselves, we want to close with some hopeful stories.

The first story is of a small Protestant church and its response to an Armenian refugee family caught in one of the most heated issues of our time, immigration. The Tamrazyan family sought asylum in Bethel Church in The Hague, Netherlands. Because Dutch law prohibits police from entering a place of worship while a service is in progress, church members organized ninety-six days of continuous worship, with the help of nearly one thousand volunteer preachers who took turns leading services. More than twelve thousand visitors came to join them. Finally, the Dutch government granted asylum to the Tamrazyans, and only then did the church service end.[7]

The second story is about the Truth and Reconciliation Commission in South Africa in the 1990s, following the end of apartheid. This was a nationwide healing process, in which whites and blacks told the truth about what had happened during apartheid. With one hand, the commission said to the perpetrators of violence, "You must tell the truth about what you did." With the other hand, the commission said, "We want you to find peace within yourself." Those who had been victims of horrific human rights violations told their stories, and those who had been the perpetrators of these violations took responsibility for their actions and asked forgiveness. This process avoided what could have been terrible violence between blacks and whites, and has been acclaimed as an example for the whole world of healing on a nationwide scale.[8]

A third hopeful story is about North Carolina Judge Lou Olivera. Joseph Serna, a veteran with PTSD, was convicted of driving under the influence of alcohol and then lied about a urine test that was part of his treatment program. Judge Olivera used the hand that says no to sentence Serna to one day in jail. He used the other hand, the one that reaches out with compassion, to drive Serna to the jail himself. Olivera saw that Serna was trembling with fear and decided to spend the night in jail with him. They sat together on the bunk and had what Serna described as a "father–son conversation."[9] Judge Olivera used the power of his position to convey compassion and solidarity to a vulnerable young man.

One of the most hopeful stories in the midst of the greatest crisis of our time, climate change, is the emergence of young activists represented by sixteen-year-old Greta Thunberg (see page xxi). Greta began in the fall of 2018 with a one-person "school strike" by sitting in front of the Swedish Parliament to protest the continued burning of fossil fuels. She decided to continue striking every Friday, and she posted what she was doing on social media. Soon the hashtag #FridaysForFuture spread, and in less than a year there were at least 1.6 million school strikers in more than 125 countries. In December 2018, Greta addressed the U.N. Climate Change Conference. In February 2019, she was instrumental in persuading the European Union to pledge one trillion dollars to address climate change during the next seven years. In the United States, young people who have been inspired by Greta are referred to as the Sunrise Generation. They comprise the largest youth movement since the 1960s, and they are resolved to make the climate crisis the central issue of U.S. politics. One young Swedish girl started all this with a one-person school strike.[10]

Finally is the story of a young boy in very different circumstances. In light of the growing concern about gun violence, which we mentioned in the Prologue, we want to leave you with hope that a nonviolent solution is always possible, even in the face of a loaded weapon. Journalist Robert Koehler writes,

> The notion that assailants are vulnerable is the key, and it contradicts the gun lobby's "beware of monsters" motif. The shooting last week at Taft Union High School bears this out. A deeply troubled 16-year-old student brought a 12-gauge shotgun to school and seriously wounded a boy in one classroom, but before he could do further harm, the teacher and an administrator succeeded in convincing him to stop shooting and hand over his weapon. "Bryan, don't shoot," the teacher said . . . the boy and his teacher stare at each other and their humanity fills the terrifying interval. "I don't want to shoot you," the boy says.[11]

When we remember who we are, as this boy did, we are all capable of empathy, altruism, and extensivity. We can all use the two hands, one to say, "Bryan, don't shoot," and the other to say, "I care about you, too." John Dear challenges us to be like Bryan's teacher, each in our own way:

> If you're alive right now, you have to be part of a global grassroots movement to stop the destruction of the planet and stop the destruction of another hundred million people this century in warfare, like we had last century. Everybody has to do their part and everybody is needed to be part of the global grassroots movement. Everybody is Rosa Parks. Your participation could make the difference. Nobody can do everything. Everybody can do something. Everybody is needed to help this become a new world of nonviolence.[12]

At the March 24, 2018, March for Our Lives, when people asked Parkland student leader Cameron Kasky, "Do you think any change is going to come from this?" Cameron said, "Look around. We are the change."

Reflection Process

1. Close your eyes and put your feet flat on the floor. Breathe slowly and deeply. Place your hand on your heart and imagine that you are breathing in and out through your heart.
2. What are your stories of hope?
3. As you continue to breathe in and out through your heart, breathe in that hope and breathe it out into the world around you, into those who need it most, and into everyone you love.

Reflection Questions

What touched me most in this chapter is . . .
When I reflect on this chapter in relation to my life, I feel . . .
I want . . .

Appendix

Peak Membership	Years	Location	Target	Type	Outcome
4,500,000	1937–45	China	Japanese Occupation	Violent	Failure
2,000,000	1978–79	Iran	Pahlavi Regime	Nonviolent	Success
2,000,000	1983–86	Philippines	Marcos Regime	Nonviolent	Success
1,000,000	1988	Burma	Military Junta	Nonviolent	Failure
1,000,000	2006	Mexico	Calderon Regime	Nonviolent	Failure
1,000,000	2005	Lebanon	Syrian Influence	Nonviolent	Success
1,000,000	1993–99	Nigeria	Military Regime	Nonviolent	Success
1,000,000	1989	China	Communist Regime	Nonviolent	Failure
1,000,000	1984–85	Brazil	Military Rule	Nonviolent	Success
1,000,000	1967–68	China	Anti-Maoists	Nonviolent	Success
1,000,000	1922–49	China	Nationalist Regime	Violent	Success
700,000	1990–91	Russia	Anti-Communist	Nonviolent	Success
700,000	1983–89	Chile	Pinochet Regime	Nonviolent	Success
550,000	1956–57	China	Communist Regime	Nonviolent	Failure
500,000	2002–3	Madagascar	Radsiraka Regime	Nonviolent	Success
500,000	1989	Ukraine	Kuchma Regime	Nonviolent	Success
500,000	2001	Philippines	Estrada Regime	Nonviolent	Success
500,000	1989	Czechoslovakia	Communist Regime	Nonviolent	Success
500,000	1963	Greece	Karamanlis Regime	Nonviolent	Success
400,000	1991–93	Madagascar	Radsiraka Regime	Nonviolent	Success
400,000	1953	East Germany	Communist Regime	Nonviolent	Failure
400,000	1941–45	Soviet Union	Nazi Occupation	Violent	Failure
340,000	1958–75	Vietnam	U.S. Occupation	Violent	Success
300,000	1990–95	Nigeria	Nigerian Regime	Nonviolent	Failure
300,000	1944	Poland	Nazi Occupation	Violent	Failure

Chart 1. Twenty-five Largest Resistance Campaigns, 1900–2006. From Erica Chenoweth and Maria Stephan, *Why Civil Resistance Works: The Strategic Logic of Nonviolent Conflict* (New York: Columbia University Press, 2011), 33.

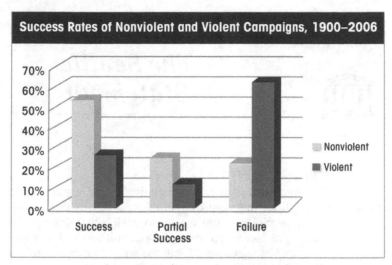

Figure 1. From Erica Chenoweth, "The Success of Nonviolent Civil Resistance," TEDx Boulder, November 4, 2013.

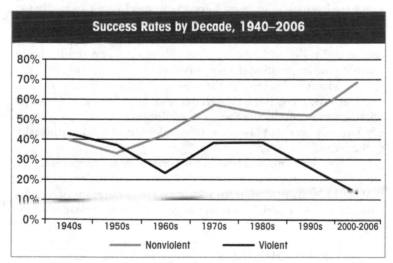

Figure 2. From Erica Chenoweth, "The Success of Nonviolent Civil Resistance," TEDx Boulder, November 4, 2013.

The Seville
Statement

INTRODUCTION

Believing that it is our responsibility to address from our particular disciplines the most dangerous and destructive activities of our species, violence and war, recognising that science is a human cultural product which cannot be definitive or all encompassing, and gratefully acknowledging the support of the authorities of Seville and representatives of the Spanish UNESCO, we, the undersigned scholars from around the world and from relevant sciences, have met and arrived at the following Statement on Violence. In it, we challenge a number of alleged biological findings that have been used, even by some in our disciplines, to justify violence and war. Because the alleged findings have contributed to an atmosphere of pessimism in our time, we submit that the open, considered rejection of these misstatements can contribute significantly to the International Year of Peace.

Misuse of scientific theories and data to justify violence and war is not new but has been made since the advent of modern science. For example, the theory of evolution has been used to justify not only war, but also genocide, colonialism, and suppression of the weak.

We state our position in the form of five propositions. We are aware that there are many other issues about violence and war that could be fruitfully addressed from the standpoint of our disciplines, but we restrict ourselves here to what we consider a most important first step.

FIRST PROPOSITION

IT IS SCIENTIFICALLY INCORRECT to say that we have inherited a tendency to make war from our animal ancestors. Although fighting occurs widely throughout animal species, only a few cases of destructive intraspecies fighting between organised

142

groups have ever been reported among naturally living species, and none of these involve the use of tools designed to be weapons. Normal predatory feeding upon other species cannot be equated with intraspecies violence. Warfare is a peculiarly human phenomenon and does not occur in other animals.

The fact that warfare has changed so radically over time indicates that it is a product of culture. Its biological connection is primarily through language which makes possible the co-ordination of groups, the transmission of technology, and the use of tools. War is biologically possible, but it is not inevitable, as evidenced by its variation in occurrence and nature over time and space. There are cultures which have not engaged in war for centuries, and there are cultures which have engaged in war frequently at some times and not at others.

SECOND PROPOSITION

IT IS SCIENTIFICALLY INCORRECT to say that war or any other violent behaviour is genetically programmed into our human nature. While genes are involved at all levels of nervous system function, they provide a developmental potential that can be actualised only in conjunction with the ecological and social environment. While individuals vary in their predispositions to be affected by their experience, it is the interaction between their genetic endowment and conditions of nurturance that determines their personalities. Except for rare pathologies, the genes do not produce individuals necessarily predisposed to violence. Neither do they determine the opposite. While genes are co-involved in establishing our behavioural capacities, they do not by themselves specify the outcome.

THIRD PROPOSITION

IT IS SCIENTIFICALLY INCORRECT to say that in the course of human evolution there has been a selection for aggressive behaviour more than for other kinds of behaviour. In all well-studied species, status within the group is achieved by the ability to co-operate and to fulfil social functions relevant to the structure of that group. 'Dominance involves social bondings and affiliations. It is not simply a matter of the possession and use of superior physical power, although it does involve aggressive behaviours. Where genetic selection for aggressive behaviour has been artificially instituted in animals, it has rapidly succeeded in producing hyperaggressive individuals; this indicates that aggression was not maximally selected under natural conditions. When such experimentally-created hyperaggressive animals are present in a social group, they either disrupt its social structure or are driven out. Violence is neither in our evolutionary legacy nor in our genes.

FOURTH PROPOSITION
IT IS SCIENTIFICALLY INCORRECT to say that humans have a "violent brain." While we do have the neural apparatus to act violently, it is not automatically activated by internal or external stimuli. Like higher primates and unlike other animals, our higher neural processes filter such stimuli before they can be acted upon. How we act is shaped by how we have been conditioned and socialised. There is nothing in our neurophysiology that compels us to react violently.

FIFTH PROPOSITION
IT IS SCIENTIFICALLY INCORRECT to say that war is caused by "instinct" or any single motivation. The emergence of modern warfare has been a journey from the primacy of emotional and motivational factors, sometimes called "instincts," to the primacy of cognitive factors. Modern war involves institutional use of personal characteristics such as obedience, suggestibility, and idealism, social skills such as language, and rational considerations such as cost-calculation, planning, and information processing. The technology of modern war has exaggerated traits associated with violence both in the training of actual combatants and in the preparation of support for war in the general population. As a result of this exaggeration, such traits are often mistaken to be the causes rather than the consequences of the process.

CONCLUSION
We conclude that biology does not condemn humanity to war, and that humanity can be freed from the bondage of biological pessimism and empowered with confidence to undertake the transformative tasks needed in this International Year of Peace and in the years to come. Although these tasks are mainly institutional and collective, they also rest upon the consciousness of individual participants for whom pessimism and optimism are crucial factors. Just as "wars begin in the minds of men," peace also begins in our minds. The same species who invented war is capable of inventing peace. The responsibility lies with each of us.

Notes

Prologue

1. "How to Stop a Fight with Pizza," https://www.youtube.com.
2. Andrew Buncombe, "Racism in the US: More Than 200 Incidents of Harassment Reported since Donald Trump Won Presidency," *The Independent*, November 12, 2016, http://www.independent.co.uk; Albert Samaha, "The Kids Are Alt-Right: Kids Are Quoting Trump to Bully Their Classmates and Teachers Don't Know What to Do about It," BuzzFeed News, June 6, 2017, https://www.buzzfeed.com.
3. Heather Dockray, "The Largest Protests in American History Are Happening Now. Expect Them to Get Bigger," Common Dreams, March 27, 2018, https://www.commondreams.org.
4. Mary Jordan and Scott Clement, "Rallying Nation," *Washington Post*, April 6, 2018, https://www.washingtonpost.com.
5. Erica Chenoweth and Jeremy Pressman, "This Is What We Learned by Counting the Women's Marches," *Washington Post*, February 7, 2017, https://www.washingtonpost.com.
6. Jordan and Clement, "Rallying Nation."
7. Ibid.
8. Fran Shor, "Spiritual Death/Spiritual Awakening," Common Dreams, March 28, 2018, https://www.commondreams.org.
9. Amy Goodman, "'I Learned to Duck Bullets before I Learned to Read': Edna Chavez at March for Our Lives Rally," March 26, 2018, Truthout, http://www.truthout.org.
10. Charlotte Alter, " "The Young and the Relentless," *Time* 191, no. 12, April 2, 2018.
11. Alter, "The Young and the Relentless."
12. Errol Salamon, "March for Our Lives Awakens Spirit of Student and Media Activism of 1960s," The Conversation, March 30, 2018, https://theconversation.com.
13. Alter, "The Young and the Relentless"; Salamon, "March for Our Lives."
14. Dockray, "The Largest Protests."
15. Jessica Corbett, "Ahead of Global #Climate Strike She Inspired, 16-year-old Greta Thunberg Nominated for Nobel Peace Prize," Common Dreams, March 14, 2019, https://www.commondreams.org.

16. Dawson Barrett, "Why the Gun Lobby Is Terrified of the Youth-Led #NeverAgain Movement," Nation of Change, March 6, 2018, https://www.nationofchange.org.

Introduction

1. Mohandas Gandhi, in John Dear, *The Nonviolent Life* (Long Beach, CA: Pace e Bene Press, 2013), 13.
2. Michael N. Nagler, *The Search for a Nonviolent Future* (Berkeley, CA: Berkeley Hills, 2001), 292.
3. Ibid., 46, 58–59.
4. James Lawson, "The Nonviolent Struggle for Justice," *Corpus Reports* 41, no. 1 (January/February 2015): 11–20.
5. Gerard Vanderhaar, *Active Nonviolence* (Eugene, OR: Wipf & Stock, 1988), 9.
6. Nagler, *Search for a Nonviolent Future*, 225.
7. Walter Wink, *Engaging the Powers: Discernment and Resistance in a World of Domination* (Minneapolis: Fortress Press, 1992), 186–92.
8. Ibid., chap. 9.
9. Mohandas Gandhi, cited in Wink, *Engaging the Powers*, 186–92.
10. Nagler, *Search for a Nonviolent Future*, 68.
11. Walter Wink, *Just Jesus: My Struggle to Become Human* (New York: Image, 2014), 140–41.
12. Ibid., 148.
13. Peter Ackerman and Jack Duvall, *A Force More Powerful* (New York: Palgrave, 2000), 365.
14. Martin Luther King Jr. and James Melvin Washington, *A Testament of Hope: The Essential Writings of Martin Luther King, Jr.* (San Francisco: Harper & Row, 1986), 18.
15. Vanderhaar, *Active Nonviolence*, 58.

Chapter 1

1. Barbara Deming, cited in Pam McAllister, *You Can't Kill the Spirit* (Philadelphia: New Society, 1988), 6–7.
2. Ibid.
3. "Disarming a Robbery ... with a Glass of Wine," https://www.youtube.com.
4. Wink, *Just Jesus*, 72–73.
5. Moises Velasquez-Manoff, "How to Make Fun of Nazis," *New York Times*, August 17, 2017, https://mobile.nytimes.com.
6. "In doubt EXIT-Germany | We Provide Ways Out of Extremism," https://www.youtube.com.
7. Velasquez-Manoff, "How to Make Fun of Nazis"; Ian Millhiser, "The Hilarious Way a German Town Turned Neo-Nazis against Nazism," ThinkProgress, August 17, 2017, https://thinkprogress.org.

8. Velasquez-Manoff, "How to Make Fun of Nazis." Quote within quote is from personal conversation of Velasquez-Manoff with Michael Nagler.

9. Ibid.

10. Greg Boyle, *Tattoos on the Heart: The Power of Boundless Compassion* (New York: Free Press, 2010), 187–212.

Chapter 2

1. Ibid., 187.

2. Walter Wink, "Why Turn the Other Cheek?" *Spirituality & Health* 7, no. 5 (October 2004): 63.

3. Allison Slater Tate, "Teen Invents 'Sit with Us' App So No High Schooler Has to Eat Alone," *Today*, September 23, 2016, http://www.today.com.

4. Adapted from Dennis Linn, Sheila Fabricant Linn, and Matthew Linn, *The Gifts of Near-Death Experiences: You Don't Have to Die to Experience Your True Home* (Charlottesville, VA: Hampton Roads, 2016), 94.

5. Yasmine Hafiz, "Samah Aidah's Soccer Team Dons Hijabs in Solidarity to Protest Referee's Unfair Treatment," HuffPost, May 12, 2014, www.huffingtonpost.com.

6. Barbara Sofer, "Not in Our Town," *Woman's Day*, November 22, 1994, 34–40.

7. Thanks to Greg Boyle for the term "solidizer," which he uses in *Tattoos on the Heart*.

8. Svati Kirsten Narula, "An Israeli Cafe Is Giving Discounts to Jews and Arabs Who Eat Together," Quartz, October 20, 2015, qz.com.

9. Kopitiam Bot, "Airbnb Is Banning People Trying to Attend a White Supremacist Rally," August 9, 2017, techcrunch.com, https://kopitiam-bot.com; Ryan J. Farrick, "Airbnb Cuts Out White Nationalists Bound for 'Unite the Right' Rally in Charlottesville, VA," August 9, 2017, http://www.legalreader.com.

10. Eleanor J. Bader, "Corporal Punishment Lives On: Students Nationwide Are Being Paddled, Restrained," Truthout, April 9, 2018, http://www.truthout.org.

11. Ashley Curtin, "Texas School District Threatens Suspension for Student Protests; Universities Respond, 'Peaceful Protests Won't Impact Admissions,'" Nation of Change, February 27, 2018, https://www.nation-ofchange.org.

12. Erica Chenoweth, "Trends in Nonviolent Resistance and State Response: Is Violence Towards Civilian-based Movements on the Rise?" *Global Responsibility to Protect* 9 (2017): 89–90.

13. Nagler, *Search for a Nonviolent Future*, 104–5.

14. Ibid.

15. Ibid., 230–31.

Chapter 3

1. Erica Chenoweth, "You Say You Want a Revolution?," UDQuickly, January 5, 2012, http://udquickly.udayton.edu; Erica Chenoweth and Maria J. Stephan, *Why Civil Resistance Works: The Strategic Logic of Nonviolent Conflict* (New York: Columbia University Press, 2011), 231.
2. Erica Chenoweth, "The Success of Nonviolent Civil Resistance: Erica Chenoweth at TEDxBoulder," November 4, 2013, https://www.youtube.com.
3. Ibid.; Chenoweth and Stephan, *Why Civil Resistance Works,* 6.
4. Chenoweth and Stephan, *Why Civil Resistance Works,* 209, 213–17.
5. Chenoweth, "The Success of Nonviolent Resistance."
6. Chenoweth, "Trends in Nonviolent Resistance," 86.
7. Ibid., 86–100.
8. Chenoweth, "The Success of Nonviolent Resistance."
9. Erica Chenoweth, "Erica Chenoweth: Morning Keynote 8/8/15—Campaign Nonviolence National Conference," PaceeBene.org, August 13, 2015, https://www.youtube.com.
10. Richard Deats, "The Revolution That Surprised the World," *Fellowship* 52 (July/August 1986): 3–4.
11. Chenoweth, "The Success of Nonviolent Resistance."
12. James L. Franklin, "A Prelate Explains 'Revolution of Love,'" *Boston Globe,* June 1, 1986.
13. Richard Deats, "One Year Later: The Nonviolent Revolution That Surprised the World," *Fellowship* 53 (March 1987).
14. Chenoweth, "The Success of Nonviolent Resistance"; Chenoweth and Stephan, *Why Civil Resistance Works,* 220–21.
15. Chenoweth and Stephan, *Why Civil Resistance Works,* 51.
16. Chenoweth, "Trends in Nonviolent Resistance," 93.
17. Ackerman and Duvall, *A Force More Powerful,* 369–71, 376.
18. Nagler, *Search for a Nonviolent Future,* 226.
19. Mark Kurlansky, *Non-Violence: The History of a Dangerous Idea* (New York: Modern Library, 2008), 148–51.
20. Chenoweth and Stephan, *Why Civil Resistance Works,* 19–20.
21. Walter Wink, *The Powers That Be: Theology for a New Millennium* (New York: Galilee, 1999), 152–53; see also Jacques Semelin, *Unarmed against Hitler: Civilian Resistance in Europe 1939–1943* (Westport, CT: Praeger, 1993).
22. Nagler, *Search for a Nonviolent Future,* 106–7.
23. Chenoweth and Stephan, *Why Civil Resistance Works,* 20.
24. Ibid., 227, 231.
25. "War since 1900—Statistics." The Polynational War Memorial, www.war-memorial.net.
26. Chenoweth, "Trends in Nonviolent Resistance," 89–90; Nagler, *Search for a Nonviolent Future,* 96–97.
27. Nagler, *Search for a Nonviolent Future,* xii–xiii.

28. Ibid., 94–95.

29. Martin Luther King Jr., in John Dear, *The Nonviolent Life* (Long Beach, CA: Pace e Bene Press, 2013), vi.

30. Chenoweth and Pressman, "This Is What We Learned."

31. Dockray, "The Largest Protests."

Chapter 4

1. Walter Wink, "The Third Way," November 14, 1993, www. cerritos.edu, Program #3707; see also Walter Wink, "Nonviolence for the Violent," Lutheran Peace Fellowship, www.lutheran-peace.tripod.com.

2. Ackerman and Duvall, *A Force More Powerful*, 3–4.

3. Gene Sharp, *Waging Nonviolent Struggle: 20th Century Practice and 21st Century Potential* (Boston: Porter Sargent, 2005), 278–79; also, "Estonia Commemorates the Baltic Chain—the Longest Unbroken Human Chain in History," *Estonian World*, August 23, 2015, http://estonianworld.com.

4. Ackerman and Duvall, *A Force More Powerful*, 6, 291, 375.

5. Nagler, *Search for a Nonviolent Future*, 114–16.

6. Kurlansky, *Non-Violence*, 20–22.

7. Ibid., 23.

8. Ibid., 35–36.

9. Ibid.

10. Ibid., 47–53.

11. Nagler, *Search for a Nonviolent Future*, 112–14.

12. Kurlansky, *Non-Violence*, 75.

13. Ibid., 77, 79.

14. Kurlansky, *Non-Violence*, 5, 75–85, 90–92; Benjamin Naimark-Rowse, "The Founding Myth of the United States of America," July 9, 2015, https://politicalviolenceataglance.org.

15. Kurlansky, *Non-Violence*, 92.

16. Ibid., 92–93.

17. Ibid., 103–4.

18. Henry David Thoreau, *Walden and "Civil Disobedience"* (New York: Signet, 1999).

19. Kurlansky, *Non-Violence*, 68–71.

20. *The Christmas Truce*, The History Channel, 2002, DVD.

21. Kurlansky, *Non-Violence*, 133.

22. *Sir! No Sir!*, produced, directed, and written by David Zeiger, 2005, DVD.

23. *Sir! No Sir!*; "GI Resistance in the Vietnam War," September 3, 2006, https://libcom.org. Resistance to the Vietnam War was largely but not entirely nonviolent. For example, there were an estimated one thousand or more instances of "fragging," in which American soldiers in Southeast Asia killed their own commanding officers. "'Frag-

ging' and 'Combat Refusals' in Vietnam," http://home.mweb.co.za/re/redcap/vietcrim.htm.

24. David Ingram, "Seattle High School Football Team Kneels for National Anthem," September 17, 2016, http://www.reuters.com; Sean Gregory, "The Perilous Fight," *Time*, October 3, 2016, 36–43.

25. Dave Zirin, "Colin Kaepernick's Teammates Give Him an Award for Courage," The Nation, January 4, 2017, https://www.thenation.com.

26. John Dear, ed., *Mohandas Gandhi: Essential Writings* (Maryknoll, NY: Orbis Books, 2002), 24.

27. Ibid., 17.

28. "India: Defying the Crown," in Steve York, *A Force More Powerful: A Century of Nonviolent Conflict* (documentary film/PBS film), 2000.

29. Ackerman and Duvall, *A Force More Powerful*, 83–90.

30. Dear, ed., *Mohandas Gandhi*, 19–32.

31. Kurlansky, *Non-Violence*, xiv.

32. Staughton Lynd and Alive Lynd, eds., *Nonviolence in America* (Maryknoll, NY: Orbis Books, 1995), 380.

33. Martin Luther King, Jr., in Lynd and Lynd, *Nonviolence in America*, 380.

34. Ibid., 385.

35. Ibid., 386.

36. Ibid., 390.

Chapter 5

1. Sarah van Gelder, "It Wasn't All Bad: Five Signs of Positive Change in 2016," *Yes! Magazine*, December 31, 2016, http://www.yesmagazine.org.

2. Matt Petronzio, "How Young Native Americans Built and Sustained the #NoDAPL Movement," December 7, 2016, http://mashable.com.

3. Laura Francis Brickman, "At the Standing Rock Reservation, Young Activists Have Been at the Forefront of Protests," October 31, 2016, https://mic.com.

4. Tom Petersen, "Why I Joined My Fellow Vets at Standing Rock This Weekend," December 5, 2016, https://www.aclu.org.

5. Van Gelder, "It Wasn't All Bad."

6. Jenna Amatulli, "Forgiveness Ceremony Unites Veterans and Natives at Standing Rock Casino," HuffPost, December 5, 2016, http://www.huffingtonpost.com.

7. Jade Begay, "Water Protectors Deliver Donations to Morton County Officers," Common Dreams, December 2, 2016, https://www.commondreams.org.

8. Yessenia Funes, "The Standing Rock Lawsuit Started a Year Ago. Here's Where We Are Now," *Yes! Magazine*, August 8, 2017, http://www.yesmagazine.org.

9. Van Gelder, "It Wasn't All Bad."

10. Ari Paul, "Seven Things the Defund DAPL Campaign Has Achieved So Far," *Yes! Magazine*, December 28, 2016, http://www.yes magazine.org; John Heltman, "Will Big Banks Pay Price for Dakota Pipeline?," American Banker, February 17, 2017, https://www.ameri-can banker.com; Colby Devitt, "Banks Have Cut Funding for Fossil Fuels Projects 22 Percent," *Yes! Magazine*, July 7, 2017, http://www.yes magazine.org.

Chapter 6

1. Walter Wink, "The Redeeming Power of the Small," *Fellowship* 66, nos. 1–2 (January 2000): 4.

2. "Nashville: 'We Were Warriors,'" in Steve York, *A Force More Powerful* (documentary film, PBS series).

3. Chenoweth and Stephan, *Why Civil Resistance Works*, 160.

4. Ackerman and Duvall, *A Force More Powerful*, 9.

5. Sharp, *Waging Nonviolent Struggle*, 27–28.

6. Ibid., 37.

7. Ibid., 29–30; Gene Sharp, *From Dictatorship to Democracy: A Conceptual Framework for Liberation* (New York: New Press, 2012), 28–29.

8. Ackerman and Duvall, *A Force More Powerful*, 86.

9. Sharp, *Waging Nonviolent Struggle*, 19, 51–65.

10. Hayley Miller, "Advertisers Ditching Laura Ingraham's Show over Attack on Parkland Survivor," HuffPost, March 30, 2018, https://www.huffingtonpost.com; Marina Fang, "Parkland Survivor Criticizes Laura Ingraham for Only Apologizing after Advertisers Fled," HuffPost, March 30, 2018, https://www.huffingtonpost.com; Ed Mazza, "Laura Ingraham Accidentally Delivered the Best Self-Own of 2018," HuffPost, April 12, 2018, https://www.huffingtonpost.com.

11. "Nashville: 'We Were Warriors.'"

12. Sharp, *Waging Nonviolent Struggle*, 44–45.

13. John Dear, interview, April 29, 2016. Used with permission.

14. Marshall Frady, cited in Nagler, *Search for a Nonviolent Future*, 52.

15. Martin Luther King Jr., "An Experiment in Love," in Martin Luther King Jr., and James Melvin Washington, *A Testament of Hope: The Essential Writings of Martin Luther King, Jr.* (San Francisco: Harper & Row, 1986).

16. John Dear, *The Nonviolent Life* (Long Beach, CA: Pace e Bene Press, 2013), 116–17.

Chapter 7

1. Nagler, *Search for a Nonviolent Future*, 214.

2. Ibid., 29.

3. Ackerman and Duvall, *A Force More Powerful*, 67.

4. Nagler, *Search for a Nonviolent Future*, 27–28.

5. Angie O'Gorman, *The Universe Bends toward Justice: A Reader on Christian Nonviolence in the U.S.* (Philadelphia: New Society, 1990), 241–47.

6. Ackerman and Duvall, *A Force More Powerful*, 74.

7. Josh Morgan, "Dakota Access Pipeline Protesters Crowdsource for $5,000, Get $1 million," CBS News, October 31, 2016, http://www.cbsnews.com.

8. Chenoweth and Stephan, *Why Civil Resistance Works*, 51.

9. Michael McLaughlin, "Dakota Access Pipeline Shooting Victim Was an Armed Instigator, Protesters Claim," HuffPost, October 28, 2016, http://www.huffingtonpost.com; Derrick Broze, "Police Violence Escalates as Provocateurs Infiltrate Standing Rock, #NoDAPL Protests," http://www.mintpressnews.com.

10. *Howard Zinn: You Can't Be Neutral on a Moving Train*, directed by Deb Ellis and Denis Mueller, 2004, DVD.

11. "It's Not Over: Daniel Sheehan on DAPL and Tigerswan," video, August 5, 2017, https://www.youtube.com; Will Griffin, "After Two Wars, Standing Rock Is the First Time I Served the American People," Common Dreams, October 30, 2016, https://www.commondreams.org; Dahr Jamail, "Missile Launchers at Standing Rock: Weaponized Law in Action," Truthout, January 27, 2017, http://truthout.org.

12. Chenoweth, "Trends in Nonviolent Resistance."

13. Tracy Loeffelhotz Dunn, "Why Police from 7 Different States Invaded a Standing Rock Camp—and Other Questions," *Yes! Magazine*, October 31, 2016, http://www.yesmagazine.org; Jenni Monet, "Sheriffs Refuse to Send Troops to Standing Rock as Public Outrage and Costs Mount," *Yes! Magazine*, November 23, 2016, http://www.yesmagazine.org.

14. Nagler, *Search for a Nonviolent Future*, 274.

Chapter 8

1. Hannah Arendt, *Eichmann in Jerusalem: A Report on the Banality of Evil* (New York: Penguin, 2006), 175.

2. Ackerman and Duvall, *A Force More Powerful*, 231.

3. United States Holocaust Memorial Museum, "Denmark," United States Holocaust Memorial Council, January 29, 2016, https://www.ushmm.org.

4. "Denmark: Living with the Enemy," in Steve York, *A Force More Powerful* (documentary film, PBS series).

5. Ackerman and Duvall, *A Force More Powerful*, 210.

6. Ibid., 210–11.

7. U.S. Holocaust Memorial Museum, "Denmark."

8. Ackerman and Duvall, *A Force More Powerful*, 210.

9. Ibid., 212.

10. Ibid., 211.

11. "Denmark: Living with the Enemy."

12. Ackerman and Duvall, *A Force More Powerful*, 215.

13. Ibid., 217.

14. Ibid., 215.

15. "Denmark: Living with the Enemy."

16. Ackerman and Duvall, *A Force More Powerful*, 220.

17. "Denmark: Living with the Enemy."

18. Ibid.

19. Philip Friedman, *Their Brothers' Keepers* (New York: Crown, 1957), chap. 12.

20. U.S. Holocaust Memorial Museum, "Denmark," https://www.ushmm.org.

21. Ackerman and Duvall, *A Force More Powerful*, 222–23.

22. Ibid., 223.

23. Ibid., 224.

24. Friedman, *Their Brothers' Keepers*.

25. Nagler, *Search for a Nonviolent Future*, 268–69.

26. U.S. Holocaust Memorial Museum, "Denmark."

27. Gerhard Sporl, "The Exception: How Denmark Saved Its Jews from the Nazis," October 17, 2013, http://www.spiegel.de.

28. Kurlansky, *Non-Violence*, 134.

29. Ackerman and Duvall, *A Force More Powerful*, 225.

30. Ibid.

31. "Denmark: Living with the Enemy."

32. Ackerman and Duvall, *A Force More Powerful*, 226–27.

33. "Denmark: Living with the Enemy."

34. Ackerman and Duvall, *A Force More Powerful*, 229.

35. "Denmark: Living with the Enemy."

Chapter 9

1. Philip Hallie, *Lest Innocent Blood Be Shed: The Story of the Village of Le Chambon, and How Goodness Happened There* (New York: Harper & Row, 1979), xvii–xviii.

2. Pierre Sauvage, *Weapons of the Spirit*, First Run/Icarus Films, 1988, DVD.

3. Hallie, *Lest Innocent Blood Be Shed,* 129.

4. Ibid., 53–54.

5. Ibid., 249.

6. Ibid., 19.

7. Ibid., 196.

8. Ibid., 203.

9. Ibid., 91.

10. Ibid., 10.

11. Ibid., 91.

12. Sauvage, *Weapons of the Spirit*.

13. Hallie, *Lest Innocent Blood Be Shed,* 173.

14. Ibid., 283.
15. Ibid., 125.
16. Ibid., 273.
17. Ibid., 160.
18. Ibid., 216.
19. Sauvage, *Weapons of the Spirit.*
20. Hallie, *Lest Innocent Blood Be Shed,* xx.
21. Ibid., 207.
22. Ibid., 216.
23. Ibid., 245.
24. Ibid., 20–21.
25. Sauvage, *Weapons of the Spirit.*

Chapter 10

1. Martin Luther King Jr. and Cornel West, eds., *The Radical King* (Boston: Beacon Press, 2016), 147.
2. "History of the SOA Watch Movement," SOA Watch, June 23, 2006, http://www.soaw.org.
3. "What Is the SOA?," SOA Watch, http://www.soaw.org.
4. "Empire Files: The U.S. School That Trains Dictators and Death Squads," with Abby Martin, The Real News Network, December 5, 2015, http://therealnews.com.
5. Linda Cooper and James Hodge, "Guatemalan Authorities Arrest SOA-Trained Officers for Massacres, Disappearances," *National Catholic Reporter,* January 11, 2016, https://www.ncronline.org.
6. Ibid.
7. Mireya Navarro, "Guatemalan Army Waged 'Genocide,' New Report Finds," *New York Times,* February 26, 1999, http://www.nytimes.com.
8. Jean-Marie Simon, "Civil Patrols in Guatemala," Americas Watch Report, August 1986, 6, https://papers.ssrn.com.
9. "SOA Trains the Military Muscle to Enforce 'Free Trade' in Latin America," SOA Watch, http://www.soaw.org.
10. "History of the SOA Watch Movement."
11. Ibid.; Roy Bourgeois, interview, May 8, 2016, used with permission.
12. Hendrik Voss, interview, April 9, 2016, used with permission; Andrea Reyes Blanco and Tim Shenk, "Land Grabbing Is Killing Honduras' People," *teleSur,* April 10, 2016, http://www.truthout.org; Arturo J. Viscarra and Michael Prentice, "Children of the Monroe Doctrine: The Militarized Roots of America's Border Calamity," SOA Watch, August, 2014, http://soaw.org; Linda Cooper and James Hodge, "Unthinkable Violence Drives Hondurans North to United States," *National Catholic Reporter,* August 18, 2014, https://www.ncronline.org.
13. Cooper and Hodge, "Unthinkable Violence."
14. Voss, interview.
15. Ibid.

Chapter 11

1. M. K. Gandhi, *The Voice of Truth: The Selected Letters of Mahatma Gandhi*, vol. 5 (Ahmedabad, India: Shantilal H. Shah, Navajivan Trust, 1969), 110.

2. Nagler, *Search for a Nonviolent Future*, 107–10.

3. Chenoweth and Stephan, *Why Civil Resistance Works*, 30–62, 220–26.

Chapter 12

1. Dear, *The Nonviolent Life*, 17.

2. Ibid., 16.

3. Anthony Doerr, *All the Light We Cannot See: A Novel* (New York: Scribner, 2014), 25.

4. Ibid., 475.

5. Jeremy Rifkin, *The Empathic Civilization: The Race to Global Consciousness in a World in Crisis* (New York: J. P. Tarcher/Penguin, 2009), 105–36.

6. Samuel P. Oliner and Pearl M. Oliner, *The Altruistic Personality: Rescuers of Jews in Nazi Europe* (New York: Free Press, 1988), xv–xix.

7. Ibid., 1.

8. Ibid., 142.

9. Rifkin, *Empathic Civilization*, 12.

10. Oliner and Oliner, *Altruistic Personality*, 173–74.

11. Peter Suedfeld and Stefanie De Best, "Value Hierarchies of Holocaust Rescuers and Resistance Fighters," *Genocide Studies and Prevention* 3, no. 1 (2008): 31–42.

12. Oliner and Oliner, *Altruistic Personality*, 176.

13. Ibid., 249.

14. Bourgeois, interview; Cooper and Hodge, "Unthinkable Violence," 24.

15. Oliner and Oliner, *Altruistic Personality*, 169.

16. Sauvage, *Weapons of the Spirit*.

17. *Gandhi*, directed by Richard Attenborough, Columbia Pictures, 1982, DVD.

18. Oliner and Oliner, *Altruistic Personality*, 177–78.

19. Ibid.

20. "Chile: Defeat of a Dictator," in Steve York, *A Force More Powerful* (documentary film, PBS series).

21. Walter Wink, "The Naked Truth: Successful Nonviolent Takeover by Nigerian Women," *Fellowship* 69, nos. 3–4 (2003): 69; "Nigerian Women / Protest Wins Oil Company Attention," *Minneapolis Star Tribune*, July 20, 2002, cited in Laura Slattery et al., *Engage: Exploring Nonviolent Living* (Oakland, CA: Pace e Bene Press, 2005), 181.

22. Slattery et al., *Engage*, 181.

23. Asawin Suebsaeng, "Right-Wing Rock Fans Get Owned by T-Shirts," *Mother Jones*, August 11, 2011, http://www.motherjones.com.

24. Nick Wing, "White Supremacist Rally in North Carolina Met by Clown Counter-Protest, 'Wife Power' Signs," Huffpost, November 12, 2012, http://www.huffingtonpost.com.

Chapter 13

1. Nelson Mandela, *Long Walk to Freedom* (New York: Bay Books, 1995), 622.
2. Michele Borba, *Unselfie: Why Empathetic Kids Succeed in Our All-About-Me World* (New York: Touchstone, 2016), 127–28.
3. David Loye, "The Ghost at the Birthday Party," Common Dreams, February 12, 2009, https://www.commondreams.org; Rifkin, *Empathic Civilization*, 91.
4. Rifkin, *Empathic Civilization*, 92.
5. Daniel Goleman, *Social Intelligence: The New Science of Human Relationships* (New York: Bantam, 2006), 55.
6. Dave Grossman, *On Killing: The Psychological Cost of Learning to Kill in War and Society* (Boston: Little, Brown, 1995), xiv–xv, 3–4, 12, 15, 17–25, 35, 180.
7. S. L. A. Marshall, cited in Alfie Kohn, *The Brighter Side of Human Nature* (New York: Basic Books, 1990), 49.
8. Ibid., 49–50.
9. Grossman, *On Killing*, 35, 250, 251.
10. Maria Santelli, "The US Military and the Myth That Humanity Is Predisposed to Violence," Common Dreams, September 9, 2015, https://www.commondreams.org.
11. Rachel M. MacNair, "Perpetration-Induced Traumatic Stress in Combat Veterans," *Peace and Conflict: Journal of Peace Psychology* 8, no. 1 (2002): 63–72.
12. Santelli, "The US Military"; Peter Van Buren, "Whistleblowers, Moral Injury, and Endless War," TomDispatch, May 18, 2017, http://www.salon.com.
13. Michael Tomasello, *Why We Cooperate* (Cambridge, MA: MIT Press, 2009), 39–41.
14. Rifkin, *Empathic Civilization*, 8.
15. Ibid., 130–31.
16. Ibid.
17. Tomasello, *Why We Cooperate*, 13.
18. Rifkin, *Empathic Civilization*, 84.
19. Goleman, *Social Intelligence*, 60.
20. Ibid., 57.
21. Ibid., 60.
22. Ibid.
23. Ibid., 61.
24. Jamil Zaki and Jason P. Mitchell, "Intuitive Prosociality," *Current Directions in Psychological Science* 22, no. 6 (2013): 469.

25. Greg Olson, "Research on Human Nature Is Cause for Optimism," *Common Dreams*, June 29, 2007, https://www.commondreams.org.

26. Summer Allen and Jill Suttie, "How Our Brains Make Us Generous," *The Greater Good Magazine*, December 21, 2015, https://greater good. berkeley.edu.

27. Goleman, *Social Intelligence*, 52.

28. Robin Karr-Morse and Meredith S. Wiley, *Ghosts from the Nursery: Tracing the Roots of Violence* (New York: Atlantic Monthly Press, 1997), 58–76.

29. James W. Prescott, "Body Pleasure and the Origins of Violence," *The Futurist* 9, no. 2 (1975): 65.

30. Ibid., 66.

31. Rifkin, *Empathic Civilization*, 60–67.

32. Inge Bretherton, "The Origins of Attachment Theory: John Bowlby and Mary Ainsworth," *Developmental Psychology* 28 (1992): 759–75.

33. Rifkin, *Empathic Civilization*, 78.

34. Oliner and Oliner, *Altruistic Personality*, 184.

35. Zaki and Mitchell, "Intuitive Prosociality," 469.

36. Gandhi, cited in Nagler, *Search for a Nonviolent Future*, 53.

37. Oliner and Oliner, *Altruistic Personality*, 162, 249.

38. Vanderhaar, *Active Nonviolence*, 84.

39. Rifkin, *Empathic Civilization*, 60.

40. Philip Zimbardo, *The Lucifer Effect: Understanding How Good People Turn Evil* (New York: Random House, 2008), 314.

41. Slattery et al., *Engage*, 142–45; see also an extensive discussion of The Milgram Experiment in Zimbardo, *Lucifer Effect*, chap. 12.

42. This section is adapted from Dennis Linn, Sheila Fabricant Linn, and Matthew Linn, *Healing the Future: Personal Recovery and Societal Wounding* (Mahwah, NJ: Paulist Press, 2012), 56–59.

43. William Peters, *A Class Divided: Then and Now*, exp. ed. (New Haven: Yale University Press, 1971). Includes an account of Jane Elliott conducting a similar experiment for adult employees of the Iowa Department of Corrections. See also the following documentary films, "The Eye of the Storm," ABC News, 1970, distributed in DVD format by Admire Productions, 2004, www.admireentertainment.com, and "A Class Divided," by Yale University Films, 1986, presented on "Frontline" and distributed in DVD format by PBS Home Video, www.pbs.org. Both programs include study guides for use with groups.

44. Peters, *A Class Divided*, 21.

45. Ibid., 24–25. A significant aspect of the experiment is how it affected learning. Jane tested the children on spelling, math, and reading two weeks before the experiment, on both days of it, and two weeks after it was over. Their scores went up on the day they were superior, down on the day they were inferior, and then stayed higher than before the experiment for the rest of the year. Jane did not understand this, and so she sent the test scores to Stanford University for evaluation. Stanford responded that it seemed as if the children's academic ability had changed in one day, but they could

not explain how this was possible. Here's how Jane explained it to herself: "On the day they are in the 'superior' group and doing genuinely superior work, they find out for the first time what their true potential is. They learn by actual experience that they can do much better work than they have been doing. . . . They don't just *think* they can do better work; they *know* they can because they have" (109–10). In other words, once the children realized that their power to learn depended on their belief in themselves, they held on to believing they were smart and didn't let go of it again. The point of this experiment is that our sense of who we are comes in large part from believing what the environment tells us about ourselves.

    46. Dear, *The Nonviolent Life*, 13.

Chapter 14

    1. Nagler, *The Search for a Nonviolent Future*, 44, 76.

    2. Mary Gordon, *Roots of Empathy* (Toronto: Thomas Allen, 2005).

    3. Borba, *Unselfie*, 3–7.

    4. Olson, "Research on Human Nature."

    5. Jean M. Twenge, "Have Smartphones Destroyed a Generation?," *The Atlantic*, September, 2017, https://www.theatlantic.com.

    6. Dr. Mercola, "Mind Hack—How Corporations Took Over Our Bodies and Brains," Mercola, September 11, 2017, http://articles. mercola.com. Based on Robert Lustig, *The Hacking of the American Mind: The Science behind the Corporate Takeover of Our Bodies and Brains* (New York: Avery, 2017).

    7. Twenge, "Have Smartphones Destroyed a Generation?"

    8. Borba, *Unselfie*, 101.

    9. Ibid.

    10. Cory Turner, "Instead of Staring at Screens, These Kids Stared at Faces," NPR, September 30, 2014, http://www.npr.org.

    11. Camillo Bica, "Deadly Games," OEN, May 7, 2009, https://www. opednews.com; Eliot A. Cohen and Dave Grossman, "On Killing: The Psychological Cost of Learning to Kill in War and Society," *Foreign Affairs* 75, no. 2 (1996): 147; Jamie Holmes, "US Military Is Meeting Recruitment Goals with Video Games—but at What Cost?," *The Christian Science Monitor*, December 28, 2009, https://www.csmonitor.com; Avril Moore, "War Is No Game, So, Why Is It Marketed to Children as One?" *Sydney Morning Herald*, June 15, 2010, https://www.smh.com.au.

    12. Michael N. Nagler, "The Cassandra Syndrome," Peace Voice, April 14, 2009, http://www.peacevoice.info.

    13. Matt Taibbi, "If We Want Kids to Stop Killing, the Adults Have to Stop, Too," *Rolling Stone*, February 16, 2018, https://www.rolling stone. com.

    14. Nagler, *The Search for a Nonviolent Future*, 92.

    15. Dear, *The Nonviolent Life*, 27, 117.

    16. Joel R. Davitz, "The Effects of Previous Training on Post Frustration

Behavior," *Journal of Abnormal and Social Psychology* 47, no. 2, Suppl. (1952): 309–15; Michael N. Nagler, "Kids & Cooperation: Daily Metta: A Natural Capacity to Cooperate," Metta Center, video, http://mettacenter.org.

17. Nagler, *The Search for a Nonviolent Future*, 9.

18. Matthieu Ricard, "Can People Change?" *Greater Good Magazine*, August 25, 2015, https://greatergood.berkeley.edu; Maria Konnikova, "Thinking Your Way to a Better Brain," BigThink, http://bigthink.com.

19. Dear, interview.

Chapter 15

1. Dalai Lama, "If Every 8 Year Old in the World Is Taught Meditation, We Will Eliminate Violence from the World within One Generation," quoted by John Bader, www.responsiveuniverse.com.

2. Malia Barca, personal communication, August 16, 2017, used with permission.

3. Doc Childre and Howard Martin, *The HeartMath Solution* (San Francisco: Harper, 1999), 28–40; Jurriaan Kamp, "A Change of Heart Changes Everything," HeartMath Institute, June 2005, 25, www.heart math.org. For the most current HeartMath research, see www.heart math.org/research.

4. Dave Grossman, "On Killing II: The Psychological Cost of Learning to Kill," *International Journal of Emergency Mental Health* 3, no. 3 (Summer 2001): 137–44.

5. Chade-Meng Tan, "Just 6 Seconds of Mindfulness Can Make You More Effective," Mindful, July 28, 2016, https://www.mindful.org; Gabriel Fisher, "Teaching Meditation to Kids in Chicago Swiftly Reduced Crime and Dropout Rates," Quartz, June 26, 2015, https://qz.com.

6. John Hagelin, "Quantum Physical Foundations of Higher States," presentation at the International Science and Consciousness Conference, Albuquerque, New Mexico, 2000; John S. Hagelin et al., "Effects of Group Practice of the Transcendental Meditation Program on Preventing Violent Crime in Washington, D.C.: Results of the National Demonstration Project, June–July, 1993," *Social Indicators Research* 47 (1999): 153–201. See also David Orme-Johnson et al., "International Peace Project in the Middle East: The Effects of the Maharishi Technology of the Unified Field," *Journal of Conflict Resolution* 32, no. 4 (December 1988): 776–812, for a discussion of the effect of prayer on the relationship between Israel and Lebanon.

7. Jurriaan Kamp, "When Monks Rule," The Optimist Daily, January/February, 2013, https://www.optimistdaily.com.

8. Ibid.; "Transcendental Meditation," http://transcendental-meditation.be/category/1-percent-effect.

9. Kamp, "When Monks Rule."

10. Ibid.

11. Nagler, "The Cassandra Syndrome."

Chapter 16

1. Oliner and Oliner, *Altruistic Personality*, 259, 260.
2. Borba, *Unselfie*, 78–80.
3. Oliner and Oliner, *Altruistic Personality*, 161.
4. James Mill, "Field of Dreams," Vimeo, Vail Mountain School, May 9, 2016.

Conclusion

1. Dear, interview.
2. Martin Luther King Jr., baccalaureate sermon at the commencement exercises for Wesleyan University in Middletown, Connecticut, 1964, quoting Theodore Parker in "Ten Sermons of Religion," 1853.
3. Dear, interview; personal communication, April 10, 2018.
4. "Nonviolence: A Style of Politics for Peace—Message for the 50th World Day of Peace," December 31, 2016, http://www.iustitia etpax.va.
5. Joshua J. McElwee, "Vatican's Second Conference on Nonviolence Renews Hope for Encyclical," *National Catholic Reporter*, April 23, 2019, https://www.ncronline.org.
6. Nagler, *Search for a Nonviolent Future*, 222–23, 254.
7 Annabelle Timsit, "A Dutch Church's 96-Day Service to Shield a Refugee Family Comes to a Happy Conclusion," *Quartz*, March 27, 2019, https://qz.com.
8. *Long Night's Journey into Day*, directed by Frances Reid and Deborah Hoffmann, California Newsreel, 2000, video.
9. Yanan Wang, "A Compassionate Judge Sentences a Veteran to 24 Hours in Jail, Then Joins Him behind Bars," *Washington Post*, April 22, 2016, https://www.washingtonpost.com.
10. Greta Thunberg, "School Strike for Climate—Save the World by Changing the Rules," video, TEDx Stockholm, December 12, 2018, https://www.youtube.com; "You Are Stealing Our Future: Greta Thunberg, 15, Condemns the World's Inaction on Climate Change," video, Democracy Now!, December 13, 2018, https:youtube.com; Julia Conley, "'Kicking Ass for Her Generation': Applause for 16-Year-Old Greta Thunberg as EU Chief Pledges $1 Trillion to Curb Climate Threat," Common Dreams, February 21, 2019, https://www.commondreams.org; Derek Royden, "The Sunrise Generation Leads the Way on Climate Action," Nation of Change, March 8, 2019, https://www.nation ofchange.org.
11. Robert Koehler, "The Empowerment Project," HuffPost, March 18, 2013, https://www.huffingtonpost.com.
12. Dear, interview.

Resources

Books

Ackerman, Peter, and Jack Duvall. *A Force More Powerful: A Century of Nonviolent Conflict* (New York: Palgrave, 2000).

Chenoweth, Erica, and Maria J. Stephan. *Why Civil Resistance Works: The Strategic Logic of Nonviolent Conflict* (New York: Columbia University Press, 2011).

Dear, John. *The Nonviolent Life* (Long Beach, CA: Pace e Bene Press, 2013).

———, ed. *Mohandas Gandhi: Essential Writings* (Maryknoll, NY: Orbis Books, 2002).

Goleman, Daniel. *Social Intelligence: The New Science of Human Relationships* (New York: Bantam, 2006).

Grossman, Dave. *On Killing: The Psychological Cost of Learning to Kill in War and Society* (Boston: Little, Brown, 1995).

Hallie, Philip P. *Lest Innocent Blood Be Shed: The Story of the Village of Le Chambon, and How Goodness Happened There* (New York: Harper & Row, 1979).

Hogg, David, and Lauren Hogg. *#Never Again: A New Generation Draws the Line* (New York: Random House, 2018).

Kurlansky, Mark. *Non-Violence: The History of a Dangerous Idea* (New York: Modern Library, 2008).

Lynd, Staughton, and Alice Lynd, eds. *Nonviolence in America* (Maryknoll, NY: Orbis Books, 1995; rev. ed. 2018).

Nagler, Michael N. *The Search for a Nonviolent Future* (Berkeley, CA: Berkeley Hills, 2001).

O'Gorman, Angie. *The Universe Bends toward Justice: A Reader on Christian Nonviolence in the U.S.* (Philadelphia, PA: New Society, 1990).

Oliner, Samuel P., and Pearl M. Oliner. *The Altruistic Personality: Rescuers of Jews in Nazi Europe* (New York: Free Press, 1988).

Rifkin, Jeremy. *The Empathic Civilization: The Race to Global Consciousness in a World in Crisis* (New York: J. P. Tarcher/Penguin, 2009).

Sharp, Gene. *From Dictatorship to Democracy: A Conceptual Framework for Liberation* (New York: New Press, 2012).

———. *Waging Nonviolent Struggle: 20th Century Practice and 21st Century Potential* (Boston: Porter Sargent, 2005).
Slattery, Laura, Ken Butigan, Veronica Pelicaric, and Ken Preston-Pile. *Engage: Exploring Nonviolent Living* (Oakland, CA: Pace e Bene Press, 2005).
Tomasello, Michael. *Why We Cooperate* (Cambridge, MA: MIT Press, 2009).
Wink, Walter. *Engaging the Powers: Discernment and Resistance in a World of Domination* (Minneapolis: Fortress Press, 1992).
———. *Just Jesus: My Struggle to Become Human* (New York: Image, 2014).
———. *The Powers That Be: Theology for a New Millennium* (New York: Galilee, 1999).

Videos

Chenoweth, Erica. "Erica Chenoweth: Morning Keynote 8/8/15—Campaign Nonviolence National Conference." YouTube. https://www.youtube.com.
———. "The Success of Nonviolent Civil Resistance: Erica Chenoweth at TEDxBoulder." TEDxTalks. YouTube. https://www.youtube.com.
The Christmas Truce of 1914. History Channel, 2002.
Freedom Riders. Directed by Stanley Nelson Jr. PBS, 2011.
Gandhi. Directed by Richard Attenborough. Culver City, CA: Columbia Pictures, 1982.
Howard Zinn: You Can't Be Neutral on a Moving Train. Directed by Deb Ellis and Denis Mueller, 2004.
Long Night's Journey into Day. Directed by Frances Reid and Deborah Hoffmann. San Francisco: California Newsreel, 2000.
Sauvage, Pierre. *Weapons of the Spirit*. Brooklyn, NY: First Run/Icarus Films, 1988.
Thunberg, Greta. "School Strike for Climate—Save the World by Changing the Rules." TEDx Stockholm, December 12, 2018. https://www.youtube.com.
York, Steve. *Bringing Down a Dictator*. Washington, DC: York Zimmerman, 2001.
York, Steve. *A Force More Powerful: A Century of Nonviolent Conflict*. Washington, DC: York Zimmerman, 1999.

About the Authors

Denny and Sheila Linn (together with Denny's brother, Matt) have taught courses on healing, forgiveness, and nonviolence in over sixty countries and in many universities, including a course to doctors accredited by the American Medical Association. They are the authors of twenty-three books, including two books for children and those who care for them. Their books have sold over a million copies in English, and have been translated into more than twenty languages.

John Linn is a college student majoring in education. He is also a children's ski instructor and camp counselor. Denny, Sheila, and John live in Colorado.

The Linns' purpose is to support personal growth and the evolution of our planet by integrating spirituality, psychology, and science in ways that empower all of us to heal personal and social wounds and discover our unique gifts for carrying out the special purpose of our lives. Their ministry is committed to the nonviolent resolution of personal and social conflicts, care for the earth, gender and racial equality, economic justice, and respect for all faith traditions. Their roots are in Ignatian spirituality, which emphasizes finding the divinity in all things.

Retreats and Conferences

For information about retreats, seminars, and conferences in English and Spanish by the authors, please contact them at (970) 476–9235, info@linnministries.org, or see their website, www.linnministries.org.

Index